ENTREPRENEURSHIP
SECRETS

BEGINNER'S GUIDE TO RUNNING A SUCCESSFUL BUSINESS

ABDUL VASI

TABLE OF CONTENTS

INTRODUCTION	1
6 WAYS TO GET THE MOST OUT OF THIS BOOK	6
CHAPTER 1	9
INSPIRE THEM BY BEING YOU	9
Honesty and transparency will always pave the way	10
Being the captain of the ship	13
Listen and support, always	15
Say thank you	16
Monkey management:	
Empower your employees to make decisions	17
Inspire by managing time efficiently	20
CHAPTER 2	25
STRENGTHEN YOUR WORKFORCE WITH GOOD PAY	25
Make every job position valuable	27
Do not forget the bonuses	29
Giving rewards is a wise policy	31
Turn top employees into shareholders	33
Losing top employees is not an option	37
CHAPTER 3	41
EMPLOYEES ARE THE KEY	41
Listen to your employees.	
Do not get blinded by Ego	43
Let go of the reins	45
Train them well and give them access	
to run your company	46

Motivate your employees to finish the work as soon as possible	50
Smart employees vs. hardworking employees	52
Growing ordinary employees into extraordinary performers	54

CHAPTER 4 — 59
HIRE SLOW AND FIRE FAST — 59

Define the job properly	63
Train them well and track their performance	64
Choose team players	66
Look for people who share your hunger	71
Get rid of dangerous elements ASAP	74

CHAPTER 5 — 79
STAFF CONFLICTS: A GREAT ENEMY OF YOUR COMPANY'S WORK CULTURE — 79

Understanding co-worker conflicts	85
Make time for employee relations	88
Resolving staff conflict: The effective ways	93

CHAPTER 6 — 99
WORRY IN BUSINESS AND HOW TO HANDLE IT — 99

Working habits to prevent fatigue and worry	101
Adding one hour a day to waking life	106
What makes you tired and what can you do about it?	109
How to eliminate 50% of your business worries	112

CHAPTER 7 — 115
STRUCTURE YOUR BUSINESS TO RUN ITSELF — 115

Simplify your business operations	119
Do not run away from delegating	121
Predict the outcomes and take necessary actions	124
Reward competence and promote healthy competition	126

CHAPTER 8 — 131
MAINTAIN RECORDS, INVEST IN TECHNOLOGY, AND IMPLEMENT WORK CULTURE — 131
Take care of the nitty gritty:
   Maintain detailed staff records — 134
Invest in technology to improve your
   employee productivity — 137
Implement holidays/work culture like the big boys — 142

CHAPTER 9 — 145
WATCH THE NUMBERS AND PAY YOUR TAXES — 145
What happens when you do not pay your taxes
   and file your returns properly? — 147
Accounting: Everything you must know — 148
Paying the taxes: A detailed guide — 152
Filing tax returns: A crucial job — 155

CHAPTER 10 — 161
OUTSOURCING TASKS, MONITORING SOFTWARE AND IP CAMERAS — 161
Outsourcing tasks: Why do you need to start
   it now? — 163
Managing software for staff monitoring:
   Why do you need it? — 166
IP cameras: A simple way to monitor the office
   and remote locations — 170

CHAPTER 11 — 175
BUILDING SUCCESSFUL TEAMS AND REDUCING WORKPLACE NEGATIVITY — 175
How to deal with workplace negativity efficiently? — 179
Building an efficient work team
   within your company — 183

RECAP — 190

INTRODUCTION

"Either you run the day, or the day runs you."-Jim Rohn, American entrepreneur, author, and speaker.

Whenever I read a book on management and entrepreneurship, there is only one thing that comes to my mind: "Does it really give you a clear picture of entrepreneurship?" In most cases, it does not. Most of the books provide you with a bunch of inspirational paragraphs along with some tips for becoming a great entrepreneur. However, they fail to provide you with real-life scenarios, and they don't make you understand the problems that you may face in your journey.

Entrepreneurship is hard! This is a truth that you need to accept at the very beginning. Of course, you will be the boss of yourself and there are several perks of being an entrepreneur but basically, it is hard and there is no denying it. The trick to becoming a great entrepreneur is not being the ideal figure that most books portray.

You can only become successful on this path if you can turn every disadvantage to your advantage. Only by tackling the tricky situations ingeniously and managing every aspect of your business carefully, you can become a successful entrepreneur.

In my career as an entrepreneur, I have come across several industrialists and CEOs. And they have told me one thing

"There is no recipe or shortcut to becoming a successful entrepreneur". You need to find out yourself the way to manage everything; overcome the hurdles and run your organization properly.

The hard thing about entrepreneurship is not to set-up an organization; choose the right niche for it and define organizational goals. The real difficult thing about Entrepreneurship is to establish a proper work culture, building a proper relationship with the employees, inspiring them to work efficiently, eliminate the negativity as well as employee conflicts and so on.

In this book, I have not written a bunch of strategies that you can follow. I have researched for months to isolate the problems that an organization generally faces; I have analyzed those problems and shared with you my experience on how to solve the problems.

This book will give you a clear idea of the problems that you are going to face and the processes that can help you to tackle this problem. However, you need to use your judgment and intelligence ultimately to achieve success. My book is just a tool that helps you to grasp the concept entrepreneurship and employee management. But you must not think of it as the greatest weapon in your arsenal to overcome all the hurdles because the weapon is you.

Now, why did I plan to focus so much on employee management in this book? Employees are one of the most vital aspects of an organization. The true strength and efficiency of your company depend completely on the perfection of your employees. If your employees do not work properly then there is no chance for your company to succeed.

I have tried to bust the myths and eliminate the misconceptions as much as I can through this book.

In my opinion, a leader is someone who walks ahead of the others and motivates the people to follow. This is the way you can take your company to the peak of success.

I have tried to cover all the points in my book as clearly as I can so that you never face any problem in understanding the facts. It does not take much effort to run your company to the ruins.

However, it takes patience and hard work to achieve success. Being an entrepreneur for more than a decade, I have faced the same problems that I have presented in this book. So, I took the liberty of sharing my experience with you in order to prevent you from making the same mistakes that I made during my beginning years.

The main idea behind writing this book is to serve as a realistic guide for you as an entrepreneur. I have prepared the topics in such a way that it increases the chances of your success greatly. The ideas, thoughts and processes involved in this book are basically targeted towards first-time entrepreneurs or the beginners who are considering of taking this entrepreneurship plunge seriously.

I think I have been able to address all the challenges, conflicts and dilemmas that you will be facing through the chapters in my book. Thorough research and years of experience that have taken the form of the chapters will be able to help you in making your entrepreneurial journey a success story.

I would like to thank my co-author Ankita Roy Choudhury who has helped me to give this book the perfect form. Also, I want to thank my editor Marcia Abramson for helping me to make all the final touches. I will always be grateful to my mother and father for always supporting me in my journey of life. My wife and three beautiful daughters have always supported and encouraged me to be strong through and thin.

It would have been impossible to make a mark for myself and so, a big thanks for being my support.

However, I would not have gained all the success without the dedication and hard work that my present, as well as past employees, had put. They are the spinal cord of my company and I will always be thankful to them for being my primary support to make my dreams come true.

I started walking on the road of entrepreneurship as soon as I graduated from college. I wouldn't say that the path I had taken was easy. I had to face losses and a lot of hurdles before becoming the successful entrepreneur that I am today. But every time I failed I gained a new experience; an experience that helped me to succeed and set my goals more efficiently.

And I have scripted all those experiences in this book to make it easy for you to understand the difficulties and formulate the strategies with utmost accuracy. This is not just a book about entrepreneurship and employee management. It feels almost autobiographical since it contains a lot of my personal stories. It almost feels like a way of looking back to the distance I have travelled since becoming an entrepreneur.

Also, it is crucial to remember that the ideas given in this book apply to the startup enterprises having 5 to 100 employees. Well, it is just the beginning as I will be coming up with a more advanced version in the near future to help out the seasoned entrepreneurs.

Now, I do not hesitate to accept the mistakes that I have made and I am not ashamed of them either. Because in my mind I know that the path that I followed and the decisions that I made will help others to make better decisions and reach even greater heights.

The road to becoming a successful entrepreneur is not a cakewalk. There will be hardships. But I am sure that this book will guide you to find the best ways to enhance the probability of achieving absolute success.

As the inspiring quote goes: **"Many people dream about being an entrepreneur, starting their own business, working for themselves, and living the good life. Very few, however, will actually take the plunge and put everything they've got into being their own boss."**- Politician Fabrizio Moreira quoted.

"So, are you up for taking the challenge of establishing a successful entrepreneurship?

6 WAYS TO GET THE MOST OUT OF THIS BOOK

- **Read and re-read:** The concepts in this book are explained thoroughly along with examples. Thus, it must not be a problem to understand the theories. Still, if you face any problem in understanding the concepts, just read the chapter, let it sink in and re-read it. Everything will become clear to you and you will start getting the meaning as well as the purpose of all the chapters.

- **Visualise the situation:** Visualising is the best way to make any concept completely clear. If you imagine and build-up an image that will make things way easier. Visualise the situations provided in the book in your mind and think about it carefully to make everything clear.

- **Brainstorm ideas:** The book is just a tool to guide you down the right path. But it requires you to brainstorm ideas and figure out the ways to implement the ideas in real-life situations. Start doing it while reading the chapter and you will be able to take the most out of this book.

- **Change the scenery to clear your head:** While you can obviously opt to read the book in one go, it is better to take it slow. The book comes with a multitude of ideas and concepts which you need to understand as clearly as possible. So, change the scenery once in a while to get the most out of this book and go ahead to gain maximum results. Ready to make a good change?

- **Have your own preferences:** It is natural to not agree with every concept you read in this book. Well, it is not mandatory to stick to the book's thoughts. So, it is better to have your own set of preferences while reading the book. When you don't agree with something, ask yourself what you mean for that will yield better results. This way you will be able to utilise the book to formulate your own strategies.

- **Challenge yourself to implement the ideas you read:** Whenever you finish a chapter, take the challenge to implement the ideas you read within a fixed time like seven days. However, it will take some time to measure the improvements as well as results. But in order to keep a track of your organisation's performance, it is necessary to keep a timely check. Follow this strategy and you will get incredible results.

1

INSPIRE THEM BY BEING YOU

"Where do you draw your inspiration from?"

I would often hear people asking me this simple question. There is no doubt that the question is simple, but I really would get fascinated by it.

"Who inspires me most?"

This question would always make me wonder. But I never got a clear answer. However, as I started walking down the path of life and gained experience, I became sure of one thing. I understood that we draw inspiration from ourselves.

Hence, another thing became very apparent to me: that I can also inspire people around me by being myself. It is a gift that we all are born with.

However, I never realized the value of this gift in real life before establishing my start-up. It had never occurred to me how important this philosophy is. But I got a glimpse of hope once I started my own company. It wasn't easy to keep the morale of my employees high all the time; especially when we used to fail.

That is when I understood that inspiration is the key! It became entirely understandable that I could not be just their boss; I would have to become something more. I needed to be the person from whom they could draw inspiration as that was the way to make my venture successful.

"Motivation is the art of getting people to do what you want them to do because they want to do it." – Dwight D. Eisenhower

I don't know whether I have become the person that can inspire my employees, but I surely try. Sometimes, I would find myself backed against the wall by the pressure of failure, and I would start connecting my thoughts piece by piece to come up with a plan for achieving success. My employees would get very excited and inspired by this, and they would start working much harder to accomplish my well-thought plan successfully.

It was then I realized that I cannot inspire my employees with interesting quotes or lectures. My motivation, my actions, and my individuality are the things that keep my employees motivated even during critical situations.

Honesty and transparency will always pave the way:

While I know that it's my actions that inspire my employees, I cannot deny that the whole concept of employee management is very daunting. There are several explanations and theories given in management books. But when you are leading a company, and several people are following every step you take, the entire process becomes much harder. Trust is the only thing that makes this process easier.

"How will you be able to manage your employees if you don't trust them?"

This was the question a friend once asked me. I failed to answer! My thoughts circled my brain, but still, it did not give me any conclusion. There was no reply to this question rather it presented me with a hidden message to decipher. Once I understood the meaning of what my friend was trying to teach me; the curtains drew apart, and everything became very clear to me. No manager can achieve glory without being honest and trusting towards employees.

With trust, honesty, and transparency, you forge an unbreakable bond with your employees. It not only inspires them, but it also helps you to taste success. So, be honest and transparent to your employees and ask them to participate in your plans to earn their loyalty.

YES! If you want to inspire and keep your employees loyal to you and your company, then you will have to be equally loyal to them. Always make them feel welcome and show them that they are an integral part of your company; your family.

"Motivation is everything. You can do the work of two people, but you can't be two people. Instead, you have to inspire the next guy down the line and get him to inspire his people." - Lee Iacocca, an American businessman.

Always remember that in a happy family everyone stays together despite all the differences. We all have our differences and similarities but what binds us all is mutual respect and trust. This is the very first lesson of entrepreneurship. Do not make your employees feel distant; show them respect and confidence to get the same back in return.

Showing your employees respect and putting their trust on you will not diminish your stature. Of course, you are the boss, and you can strategize or execute the plan from your office. But can you do it successfully without the help of your employees?

A clear No! You can't! You can order your employees to do things without explaining anything but will that be of any help? I guess not! It's not possible to work on anything if you do not have a clue of what it is about.

"How will I feel if someone asks me to do work without explaining why?"

My mind has always wondered when someone has told me to stop being so friendly to my employees. I have also been advised not to share my plans with my employees. And every time I faced such situations, I could not help imagining how the employees would feel. I visualized myself running through a forest with my eyes blindfolded. This was depressing! Hence, I was very transparent about keeping my employees well aware of everything to keep them motivated so that they could do their work efficiently.

I think my transparency and friendly attitude towards my employees helped in making my business processes much more efficient. As I said earlier, my company is my big, loyal family! So, if you always maintain your distance from employees, if you do not share what you are planning and how you are going to achieve it, then they will never be able to put their trust in you.

And trust me, it is vital to gain the confidence of the employees. I consider the key is to be transparent and honest with your employees. Disclose plans to them, ask them for their suggestions and be frank with them about everything.

This will make them feel connected with you and your company. The barriers that can arise due to miscommunications between entrepreneur and employees will not develop. Thus, you will be able to keep the complications far away from yourself.

Being the captain of the ship:

I know for sure that keeping everything less complicated is daunting but leading employees in the right direction is tough on a whole new level. Tell me, have you ever met the captain of a ship? Surely, the captain does not do everything himself, but he (or she!) surely does lead the crew from the front. You are a captain too but not of any actual ship; rather you are the leader of your company.

This is something important that needs to be done to keep employees motivated and charged up. In every company, each employee has their own responsibilities. Hence, each of them faces different problems. Even though they try to solve everything, there are a few problems that become too difficult for them to handle.

On a ship when crew members come across any unprecedented situation, the captain comes to their rescue. He suggests everything that needs to be done to save the ship from sinking and comes out victorious at the end of the day!

Are you doing the same thing with your employees? Do you have their back whenever they are in the midst of a heap of problems or do you order them to figure out the solution themselves?

"Sir, this customer is asking for a special discount. What should I say?"

Often someone would always come running to my cubicle with such problems. My employees know that I am always there to be their light that guides and helps them to cross the sea of unwanted problems smoothly. I am accessible and they can come to me with their problems without having to worry about anything. And I am very grateful for having such camaraderie with my employees.

"Ultimately, leadership is not about glorious crowning acts. It's about keeping your team focused on a goal and motivated to do their best to achieve it, especially when the stakes are high and the consequences really matter. It is about laying the groundwork for others' success, and then standing back and letting them shine." – Chris Hadfield, Canadian astronaut

Actually, if I don't maintain good relations with my employees and do not make myself available, then why would they feel the zeal to work properly? Every time you step in to help them out with their problems, you project yourself as one of them. You become the person whom they can look up to for getting help.

This is what a captain does! It makes you a role model to your employees and they start respecting you from their heart. Above all, it helps employees to get motivated and inspired to do their work.

What happens if you make yourself unavailable whenever your employees are facing any problem?

Now, how can I put it in the best way? Okay, let's turn back the clock and visit our school days. Do you remember how frustrated you used to get when you could not solve a certain math problem even after several tries? It used to strip you of all your enthusiasm for math and your hatred for the subject would increase undoubtedly.

You must be wondering about the connection between boring math problems and motivating your employees. If math could have destroyed your enthusiasm, don't you think it is natural for employees to feel unenthusiastic if you fail to become their guiding light?

They lose interest as well as motivation and ultimately indifference grows in them about their work. Do they become the losers then? I hope not! As an entrepreneur, if you fail to motivate and inspire your employees, you fail to manage your employees.

Since there is no room for failure, be the captain of the ship and lead your crew from the front. Be there always to help your employees out and stand by their side firmly. It will help them get motivated, it will help them work hard and take you to the peak of success.

Listen and support, always:

You can never become a good leader to your employees if you don't listen and support them when they need your aid most. We learn to walk with support from our parents. Without their help, it is not possible for us to learn the basic things. Similarly, every employee needs your support to give their best at work. Everything becomes much more interesting when we know that there will always be someone who will be our primary support in our workspace.

And it is your duty to become the certain someone who will support them when they need it. The employees also want their boss to listen to their ideas. This does not get them anything glorious but it motivates them enough to work without backing down.

"You'll attract the employees you need if you can explain why your mission is compelling: not why it's important in general, but why you're doing something important that no one else is going to get done." – as said by Peter Thiel in his book Stack It Up!: Stop Losing Talent; Build the Next Level Together.

When employees receive motivation from you, you move one step closer to achieving success. As an entrepreneur, I also follow this simple rule. Often my employees come to me with new ideas or plans for a new campaign that I can run on my website. No matter how unlikely their ideas are, I manage time to listen to them and support their ideas valiantly.

I do not get paid for being valiant or for listening to them! But when they come to me with an exciting idea, they get much more inspired and charged after I make a simple appreciation for the way they are thinking of the company as their own. They work harder and formulate excellent plans which actually earn a profit for my company.

If you really want to gain profit then you must understand this pivotal aspect of human nature. Always be there to give proper praise to employees whenever they achieve something. It will not only give them happiness but it will inspire your employees in such a way that they will be able to excel in their work.

If you keep your employees happy and inspired then you will never have to look back. Do not try to be the boss or an efficient entrepreneur! Be yourself; be the one your employees will be able to relate to. There is no pride in proving yourself superior to your employees; rather try to be one of them.

You are the person who is best fitted to motivate and inspire employees. Stop masquerading as someone else; be the person you are and listen, support and stand by your employees always.

Say thank you:

Supporting and listening to clients undoubtedly is a great motivator but sometimes all it takes is just a little "thank you" to motivate employees. No! I am not joking about this. This is something my years of experience as an entrepreneur has taught me. Often I find someone running errands for me. I see how hard they work in order to get a little recognition from me.

So, upon finishing the work, when I thank them, I can vibe the joy and pride that they feel deep down. What will I get by making them happy? Surely, it won't earn me anything but I will definitely profit from it in the long run.

How will I profit by making my employees happy?

Well, happiness is a great motivator. When I am thanking my employees, it shows how grateful I am for the services that they provided me. It shows that I am evaluating their performance and keeping a close track on whatever they do. But above all, it helps them believe that they can receive praise from me and it is also feasible to earn a special place in my eyes if they work properly. In my opinion, this is enough to motivate any individual to continue their good work.

Monkey management: Empower your employees to make decisions:

It is important that I thank my employees for everything they do and always stand by their side, but there are some times when employees must make their own decisions instead of running to my cubicle. What I learned from my personal experience is that I need to pass the monkey.

Well, I am not talking about passing an actual monkey to my employees! It is a common phrase in the world of management. Actually, what helped me to empower my employees to make their own decisions is "monkey management."

Theodore Roosevelt once said: **"The best executive is the one who has sense enough to pick good men to do what he wants to be done and self-restraint enough to keep from meddling with them while they do it."** And it forms the ground of the concept of monkey management.

So, what is monkey management? How do I do it?

Actually, monkey management is about passing the unnecessary burdens. As an entrepreneur, I have much important work to complete. I cannot meddle in every affair; otherwise, important tasks will get delayed. This is the exact point where monkey management comes in.

Back in 1974, an article was released in the Harvard Business Review by **William Oncken Jr.** and **Donald L. Wass.**

In the article, the duo took a unique approach towards solving managerial problems. They termed the problems as monkeys, which gave rise to the concept of monkey management.

Oncken and Wass wrote: **"The unsolved problems are like 'monkeys.' And the managers are unwittingly reducing their effectiveness by taking ownership of monkeys that rightfully need to stay with the employee."**

I can completely relate to what Oncken and Wass said in their article. I would often find employees running to my cubicle in order to ask me everything.

"Sir, our printers are not working properly. Should I ask the IT professional to get it checked?"

Employees would always come to my cubicle with such problems. And I could not do anything other than help them out. But it really became very problematic for me, since it would deter me from the work that I was doing. I could not focus hence I was failing badly to adhere to my deadlines. At times, I used to feel very helpless. Luckily, one day I came across the article about monkey management. "Bingo!" I cried in my mind as I finally knew that I had found something to reduce the burden on my shoulders.

And I employed the technique successfully in my workspace. So, what did I do? How did I get rid of the monkeys? Now, it is never good to drive the employees away. It will make them feel helpless. As I stated earlier, listening to and supporting the employees is necessary for motivating them. So, I could not just drive them away. Rather I came up with an innovative approach.

The approach was very simple indeed. I empathetically listened to everyone who came to my cubicle with their problems. If it was something that I could not bear to spend my time on, then I would simply tell the employee: "Okay! So what do you need me for? You are the person for the job. I trust that you will be able to handle this better than me. Relax! I believe you will be awesome at performing this task."

By saying such simple things to employees, I killed two birds with one stone. I prevented the breeding of a monkey and I made my employees believe that they have what it takes to make the decisions themselves. I installed the thought in their heads that they do not need my help for everything. There are things that they can carry out themselves.

As I successfully made my employees believe that they can solve minor problems without my help, it helped me to increase my work efficiency by not meddling in unimportant things. But above all, it helped my employees to believe in themselves and get motivated.

Blaine Lee, an American author, once said in a conference: **"The great leaders are like the best conductors – they reach beyond the notes to reach the magic in the players."** That is what I aimed for with the monkey management technique. My goal was to free myself so that I could do the important work without solving others' problems. But above all, I planned to bring out the best in my employees by empowering them.

Since everything went as I planned, I can now feel the difference. I no longer get deterred from my work and my employees have become more efficient. They no longer run to my cubicle for help rather they make the decision unless it is too important not to bring to my notice. And this certain sense of authority also motivates them to perform well. Inspire employees to make their own decisions and bring a proper balance of work in the workspace.

Inspire by managing time efficiently:

Now that the monkey is successfully shoved off from your shoulders, let me tell you another secret. Managing time is as important as managing monkeys. But how does it relate to inspiring employees? Actually, it has everything to do with inspiring employees. As I have said before, employees take their inspiration from looking at their boss. So, if I manage my time, if I meet my deadlines efficiently then it will lead employees to do the same.

I spend every second very carefully and it transcends to my employees. Once I read a quote from author and speaker **Michael Altshuler: "The bad news is time flies. The good news is you're the pilot."** So, I had to take the steering of time in my own hands. Time is very important in every organization.

Thus, it is the goal of an enterprise to make the most out of the time available. And that completely depends on how employees manage their time. But unless they see their boss doing so, the concept will never be clear to them. This is something that occurred to me after I hopped on the journey of entrepreneurship.

Yes! I was not excellent at managing my time before I became an entrepreneur. All my life I have heard about time management. In my childhood often I would find my elders saying: **"Time

and tide wait for no man." I was really reluctant. I would always wake up late in the morning and would spend the most of the night working. It did not affect me much during my teenage days, but as I started my own company I realized that I needed to change my habits. And there is an interesting story behind it!

During the early days of my company, I used to come to the office at 9 a.m. I felt more comfortable working late at night and coming to the office a little late. So, I planned my office time from 9 a.m. to 6 p.m. as per my convenience. But it did not work out well! I found out that my employees were not walking on the path of punctuality.

They were coming to the office late and it was truly hampering my business. As they were coming late to the office, it was becoming hard for them to execute the work within deadline. I felt perplexed! I didn't know what I needed to do to put a stop to it and the work culture in my office was getting destroyed.

One day I was reading **Victor Hugo** to get rid of my perplexity when I came across a particular quote: **"He who every morning plans the transaction of the day and follows out that plan carries a thread that will guide him through the maze of the busiest life. But where no plan is laid, where the disposal of time is surrendered merely to the chance of incidence, chaos will soon reign."** It really struck me and all at once I realized that I needed to change myself first.

In order to change myself, I started hitting the bed early and I turned myself into an early riser from a late owl. I started waking up at 4 a.m. Once I began starting my day at 4 a.m., I felt a change in me. I became more proficient at handling work pressure and started making decisions with a clear head. The cool morning breeze and serenity of the dawn helped me come up with new ideas to take my business forward. And the work culture at the office? Yes! By becoming an early riser, I solved that problem too.

As I became an early riser, I was able to start my office time from 7.30 a.m. I would come to the office first, at 7.30 A.M sharp, and would work till everybody left. After a few days, I noticed a sudden change in my employees. They were becoming punctual. Everybody started entering the office space right at 8 o'clock and began working without any delay. Since then I have never found any employee entering the office late. It really boosted the efficiency of work and provided me with the opportunity to achieve new business goals.

It is true that this time management trick helped to achieve lucrative business goals, but it also really helped me to organize myself. Moreover, it solidified my belief that it is my actions that ultimately inspire my employees. So, it is important to start the day early as it offers so many advantages. And I think all the top CEOs will agree with me on this point.

Of course, they will agree with me since they always inspire everyone to start the day early as it helps in managing time properly. I read an interview with Apple CEO **Tim Cook** in a magazine where he said that he wakes up at 4:30 a.m. It helps him to plan his work properly and finish the work as planned. Well, I cannot expect any less from the man organizing the most valuable company in the world.

Not only Tim Cook but Starbucks CEO **Howard Schultz** is also an early riser. He wakes very early in the morning and reaches the Starbucks headquarters within 6-6:30 a.m. Disney CEO **Bob Iger** is also a part of this club as he wakes up at 4:45 a.m. The point of saying this is that these most successful executives are waking up early, and they are not only managing their time intelligently but they are also setting an example to follow. And it is the responsibility of an entrepreneur to set an example in front of employees.

Set yourself as an example; always be the person that you are. It is you who have the power to encourage and inspire your employees. Believe in yourself. Only then will your employees get inspired by you.

SECRET 1

Always treat your employees as you treat your best clients; it will help them to get inspired and play their part with utmost efficiency.

So, what are you doing to inspire your employees?

2

STRENGTHEN YOUR WORKFORCE WITH GOOD PAY

"Am I paying my employees well?"

This is one of the few things that every sensible entrepreneur worries about. It is true that the best way in which I can motivate my employees is by being my own self. But is it possible to keep that motivation up if I do not compensate my employees well? In reality, that is not possible! Money is something that everyone requires.

No matter what I want to do, I will need money. Even the ultimate goal of my business is also to earn more money by maximizing my profits. So, is it really sane to think that my employees will stay with me if I fail to pay them well?

No! They will never stay with me. It will bring their morale down and my company will descend into nothingness. I often hear people giving lectures about customer satisfaction and different ways to make your customers happy. Well, it is undoubtedly important but that is not all.

A company is like a family. If the bonds within this family are not strong enough then it is never possible to satisfy the customers or earn profits. My employees are ultimately doing the job to earn a good livelihood and as an employer, it is my duty to provide them with that. I can motivate them by treating them well or listening to them, but to keep the motivation up a good payroll structure is always needed.

Right! A good payroll structure is always required because that is what ultimately matters. I grasped this concept after I started my journey as an entrepreneur. I understood how valuable a good pay structure can be in a company.

Theodore Roosevelt once said, **"Appraisals are where you get together with your team leader and agree what an outstanding member of the team you are, how much your contribution has been valued, what massive potential you have and, in recognition of all this, would you mind having your salary halved."** Even though he said it almost a century ago, its meaning is still relevant in our society. I have always wondered whether I am doing everything in my power to compensate my employees but I know that I surely try.

Of course, I try to pay them a good salary, provide them with hefty bonuses during special occasions and serenade them with incentives whenever they achieve something praiseworthy. Employees are the lifeline for every company. So, if they are not happy, if they are not working efficiently then it is never possible to achieve the business goals that we have planned for so long.

Life is always not so easy and money is something that helps to assure everyone a stable and settled life. I might not be able to solve all the problems that my employees face but I can surely provide them with a good chance to fight their financial instabilities with a good pay structure. And this is something that may not matter the most but surely helps to secure your employee's life.

Make every job position valuable:

Undoubtedly, framing a good salary structure is one of the crucial things that I can do as an employer. However, I cannot just pay any amount of money as wages. Everything has a system and formulating a justifiable pay structure has to be done systematically too.

Is it really important to have a good pay structure? Everything can work just fine without one!

Before I continue with how to be systematic while creating a pay structure, let me make this very clear for you. Obviously, I can pay my employees any amount without following any pay structure but that will never work out. A good pay structure is not just about salary. There are several other things that are included which makes it so effective.

The effectiveness of a good pay structure can be understood by some simple facts. It has been found in many studies that the rate of employee retention and satisfaction increases greatly when a company has an efficient pay structure. It is only natural given the fact that a good salary, bonuses and extra incentives can act as a great motivator, at least in the short term.

Though it is not a great motivator in the long run, still it can boost the morale of anyone on any given day.

Pastor **Sunday Adelaja** said in one of his books,"**A salary does not make a person rich, but only gives him the opportunity to take care of his needs. It is not a means of becoming wealthy. It is a means of fulfilling our potential.**"And it is still motivating me to do right by my employees; to salute their potential and the hard work that they do.

As saluting is not enough, now it is time to ponder how to create a stable salary structure for employees. The very first thing that needs to be done is to make every job position valuable. Whenever I am hiring people for my company, they always look out for what they will be getting. What is in the job for the employees is the first thing that motivates them to take the job and do it earnesty. Now, this is something for which an entrepreneur must do proper research.

Without proper research, it is never possible to add a respectable value to job positions. Back when I was recruiting my staff, I remember that I used to research a lot to determine a good wage structure for my company. So, what kind of research will it be? Well, this is something similar to market research. Prior to any other task, I started identifying my competitors in business.

Wait, what? Why will I need to identify my competitors to create a sta ndard pay scale for my employees?

Identifying the competitors in the business is necessary to understand the standard or benchmark wage for a particular job position in the market. As an employer, I will always have to maintain the standard benchmark. In any case, I cannot pay them less since it will reduce the value of the job position.

However, I can actually pay the employees a little more to make my job offers much more appealing. If the employees see that they are getting more value by working for me then it will obviously charge them up to work for me and to work earnestly to avail the incentives that come with the job.

Once in an interview, **Alfred Hitchcock** said, **"When an actor comes to me and wants to discuss his character, I say, 'It's in the script.' If he says, 'But what's my motivation?' I say, 'Your salary.'"** It may sound little rude but what the legendary filmmaker tried to convey was correct.

And I can understand its accuracy by my own experience. At the beginning of my journey as an entrepreneur, I used to pay my employees on the basis of the work they were doing. But I could feel that something was off. They did not have the tenacity to work hard and efficiently. Moreover, the thing that had struck me most was that I was not getting good responses from the advertisements that I had posted for job vacancies.

Later, I found that the wage that I was offering was not par for the market standard. Hence, I researched, prepared a good salary structure and now I have the best employees who work hard to achieve my organizational goals. So, creating a good salary structure is a priority and soon, the changes will start to surface.

Do not forget the bonuses:

While it is important to have a standard salary structure, it is far more important to give bonuses.

What! Do I need to pay them a bonus? But why is it so important?

Of course, it is very crucial to give bonuses at the right time. Bonuses act like vitamin supplements for employees. They are not a part of the salary rather the bonuses are extra incentives that an employer gives to employees as a token of appreciation for all the work they do. And what can employers expect in return? To be very specific, in return, giving bonuses keeps morale high. It motivates employees to deliver their best for bagging some appreciations and bonuses.

The famous American author and speaker **John C. Maxwell** once said, "**How do leaders serve their people? They may pay good wages and treat employees with respect.**"And paying good bonuses is a great way to show employees respect and serve them well.

Speaking of paying good bonuses, there is a great analogy that can be drawn. In my childhood days, whenever my uncle would come to our house, he would give me some money to buy chocolates. This was something that he would do out of the goodness of his heart, even if it was not needed. But when he would give me the money with a big smile on his face, I could feel my heart beating faster with happiness. Irrespective of the amount, the idea of getting the gift would make me happy.

After all these years, when I look back at those days, I can understand that my employees feel the same thing when I give them bonuses. The bonuses basically bring happiness to the employees and show them that their boss has faith in them. Moreover, it strengthens the bond between the employer and employees.

In order to strengthen and express my love towards them, I give bonuses to my employees on special occasions or during festive seasons. Everybody likes gifts during the holidays and I seize this opportunity to gift my employees with bonuses. From my experience, I can surely say that this trick always works. Every time the bonuses are credited to the accounts of my employees, they get recharged with extra energy and the efficiency of their work increases. And the effect remains until the staff gets their next bonus.

Happiness is something that must be shared with everyone. I am making money from my business but the people who work for me are contributing greatly to this success. It is because of them that all my dreams are gaining the shape of reality. And it would be inhumane if I failed to appreciate it. So, with the bonuses, I can always tell them how important they are to me and to my company. Plan the bonuses well and give them to the employees timely to ensure a harmonic progression of your success graph.

Giving rewards is a wise policy:

Now, are you planning to start with the bonus policy? You must, as it's a great way to inspire employees and retain their focus on the job. With bonuses, you can show how much you care about them. But what should be done when they achieve something or perform outstandingly? Or when they have won over some impossible clients? How do you reward employees during such circumstances?

The simplest thing that can be done is to give them salary increments or monetary rewards when they have achieved something extraordinary.

In his book People Glue, **Ian Hutchinson** wrote, "**Your number one customers are your people. Look after employees first and then customers last.**" I find this quote very educational because I feel it expresses the most basic essence of what it means to be an entrepreneur.

To be an entrepreneur means to understand that you can never achieve anything alone. Even though I am the boss and everything that happens is because of my plans and dreams, I would not be able to accomplish anything without the hard work of my employees. This is something that every employer must never forget.

So, it is essential to reward and celebrate the extraordinary achievements of employees since it gives them good vibes and motivates them to work even harder. It presents employees with the idea that if they work hard then they can acquire incredible rewards. And don't forget, your employees will be determined to produce the best.

How can I reward my employees? What can I do to charge them up?

The goal is always to give employees the idea that if they work hard then they can achieve rewards apart from recognition. And as I have stated before, there is no greater motivator than money. People work hard and get a job just to live a comfortable and happy life. So, it is always the primary motivation for employees.

They always look out for the ways in which they can earn salary increments or promotions; so that they can have a better shot at life. As an employer, it is my duty to keep track of their performance and reward them with increments or bonuses when they truly execute a commendable job and perform outstandingly.

While we are talking about rewarding employees with bonuses or increments, I have an interesting story to share. It is from the time when I had just started my company. In those days, sales were very low as I was just beginning my path towards success. One day I learned that one member of my team had acquired ten new customers for the company on a single day. I was naturally very thrilled. I congratulated him heartily and asked him to keep up the good work.

However, I could feel there was a little unhappiness lurking at some corner of his mind. I was lost in thought about how I could increase the meter of excitement. Then, the quote from Ian Hutchinson started to linger in my mind. Finally, I decided to reward him with an increment on his salary and that was unquestionably one of the best decisions I ever made.

Since that day, he has always been one of the most dedicated staff members in my organization. The secret to success for any organization lies in satisfying the employees. And this incident gave me a great idea about how to maintain employee satisfaction by giving rewards. So, I developed my own way of rewarding my employees.

Yes! I developed an effective trick to reward my employees to keep their motivation high. The performance of my employees is evaluated on a monthly basis and I name the employee having the best performance as the employee of the month. The employee of the month receives a certain amount of money as a compliment for good work. And the employee who is nominated for employee of the month the most times gets a chance to win the employee of the year award which includes a salary increment and better monetary allowances.

This motivates them to work earnestly throughout the year and serve my company's purpose well which helps me to achieve my goals successfully. So, do not hesitate to spend money to give rewards because as marketing and organizational expert **Sybil F. Stershic** said, "**The way your employees feel is the way your customers will feel. And if your employees don't feel valued, neither will your customers.**"

Turn top employees into shareholders:

The way you make your employees feel will always affect your customers' views towards your company. This is something that I have already told you. But what other way is there to make your employees feel connected with your organization? Well, I have a plan! I can turn my top employees into shareholders which will boost their morale.

Am I serious? Or is it a farce?

An entrepreneur must use different ways to retain employees and boost their efficiency. So, it was not a joke. Employees can be turned into shareholders and there is no way that you will face any trouble for that. As the famous actress **Audrey Hepburn** once said, **"Nothing is impossible, the word itself says, 'I'm possible!'"** Therefore, there is no point in thinking that it will be an irrational thing to do. As I have said before, employees are the lifeline of an organization.

Hence, it is always my primary goal as an entrepreneur to make them happy and satisfied. They work hard every day as I do and they give their all to the company that I am running. Thus, if they do not get rewarded with what they deserve then it will obviously destroy their faith in me and will turn them away from the company. If there is anything that I have learned as an entrepreneur, it is the simple concept that skillful employees are real treasures and I cannot let them leave at any cost.

As I am unwilling to let skillful employees leave, I will have to implement perfect strategies to increase the rate of employee retention. **Anne M. Mulcahy,** the former CEO and chairperson of the iconic Xerox Corporation, once said in an interview: **"Employees are a company's greatest asset – they're your competitive advantage. You want to attract and retain the best; provide them with encouragement, stimulus, and make them feel that they are an integral part of the company's mission."** So, even if it means that I have to turn my employees into shareholders there is nothing wrong with it.

Furthermore, turning the employees into shareholders is an ingenious move. The profit, loss and growth of a company are the liabilities of the shareholders. So, if you assign some percentage of the total share to an employee, then it will only motivate them to increase their effort and dedication to their work in order to achieve the business goal of the company.

But reaching the point where employees will be fully dedicated to achieving the business goals is not easy. There are a few things that always need to be taken care of before turning an employee to a shareholder. The first question that comes to my mind is whether it is legal. The answer completely depends upon the type of company. If it is a private limited company, then there are limitations which will have to be carefully followed.

In order to turn an employee to a shareholder, the first thing that will be required in a private limited company is the permission of the board of directors. If the board approves then it can be done easily. However, if it is a private company, then there is no need to get approval from a board as the power of making such decisions always rests with the entrepreneur.

Now that I have explained the legal concerns, it is time for me to discuss the second most important thing. **How will I select the employee?** In most cases, it would be obviously foolish to turn all the employees into shareholders, so there must be a scale that needs to be followed. In my opinion, the employee who deserves to be a shareholder of my company has to be the one with consistent performance and skills.

What do I mean by that? I mean that the performance of the employees must always be considered in judging who deserves to be a shareholder. I remember having a conversation with a friend on this topic. I asked him, **"How will I select the employee? How will I know who deserves to be a shareholder of my company?"** The reply that my friend gave me is one of the best pieces of advice that I have ever received.

My friend calmly said in reply, "**Always identify the employee who has the most consistent performance and skill sets that your company requires. Find the one who will affect the productivity of your organization the most if he decides to leave. That is the asset that you must never lose. Give him some shares and keep him associated always with your company.**" When I think back and remember his words, I can understand how true they were.

Hence, the employees who are most valuable to the organization are the ones who must be turned into shareholders. **But how many shares should they be given?**

As one problem gets solved, another presents itself. It is essential to determine the percentage of shares that will be given to the selected employee before finalizing the deal. It is foolish for entrepreneurs to harm their own position in the company in order to please employees. Giving too much of a share will provide the employee with unwanted power which may ultimately harm the company.

So, the percentage always has to be nominal. I think it is always best to give 5-7% of the share to each of the top employees in order to make them shareholders.

As I speak of giving a 5-7% share to the top employees, I must also think from their perspective. What will the employees get if I make them shareholders with 5-7% share? I have already talked about motivation and similar issues. But what will really compel them to accept this offer? Well, it is the extra income that they will generate from the share. Having a 5-7% share of the company is enough to provide them with a good amount other than their basic salary. And as I have always said there is no greater motivator than money.

Furthermore, the amount that they get will always depend on the profit that the company generates. So, it will always motivate them to work hard, innovate and find new ways to ensure sustainable growth for the company.

In the words of **Herb Kelleher,** the CEO of Southwest Airlines, **"Your employees come first. And if you treat your employees right, guess what? Your customers come back, and that makes your shareholders happy. Start with employees and the rest follow from that."** So, do the thing that needs to be done, turn the most valuable employees into shareholders and ensure success for the organization.

Losing top employees is not an option:

Since I have already discussed that turning employees into shareholders is a wise policy, it must also be remembered that losing a talented employee is not an option. **"When leaders throughout an organization take an active, genuine interest in the people they manage, when they invest real time to understand employees at a fundamental level, they create a climate for greater morale, loyalty, and, yes, growth"** this is something that management consultant **Patrick Lencioni** once said and it has always acted as a great motivator for me.

So, if it means giving into the demands of salary increments or bonuses of the top employees, then an entrepreneur must do so.

Yes! An entrepreneur might have to give into the demands of the most talented employees if it becomes the need. And I have learned it from my own experience as an entrepreneur. The concept of employees being the greatest asset to a company was not very clear to me at the beginning.

Well, I used to do everything I could to please my employees but the concept of giving in to their terms was not acceptable to me. But everything became clear in the end. And how I understood the importance of retention of top employees is a beautiful story which I am going to share.

Once I had an employee who used to outsmart most of his colleagues with his talent and brilliant performance. He had worked three years for me and he was leading the sales generation for my company. One day as I was sitting in my cubicle, suddenly he came to me. He informed me that he wanted to pursue a different career. I knew that there was more to it than what he was saying. So, I asked him what problem he was facing and what I would have to do to retain a talented employee like him.

At last, after much prompting, he said that he was unhappy with his salary and asked for an increment. Much to my dismay, he demanded to double his salary. I was little egoistic and I would never give into such an absurd demand. So, I explained everything to him and tried to convince him that his demands were absurd. But our negotiations did not work and he left the company.

A few months later, I was in an event of my vendors' team. I was having a nice conversation with one of my Account Manager - **Muktadir Syed.** Suddenly, he asked me about the employee who had left my company after I refused to accept his demands. I told him everything that had happened.

He turned towards me and said: "**Abdul, efficient employees like him are your biggest asset. Do not lose them! Losing talented employees will only bring harm to your business. One talented employee is efficient enough to do the work of three employees. So, even if it means to pay them extra then do not hesitate, as you will only be making a profit.**"

I instantly understood how foolish I was and the mistake I made. Hence, I vowed to retain talented employees at any cost. And I even convinced the ex-employee to rejoin my company by offering him a good salary package. Therefore, you can understand that even if you pay these talented employees more, you are investing in the right thing and good investments always give good paybacks. Do not lose talented employees, understand what they want, pay them well and ensure optimum business growth.

SECRET 2

Offer employees a good salary structure with allowances and bonuses; it will always keep them loyal.
What are you planning to do to strengthen your workforce?

3

EMPLOYEES ARE THE KEY

My friend once asked me, "What is the secret behind building a successful company?" back when we were just college graduates.

Yes, I was an ambitious young man but definitely was too very confident to see the reality.

I slammed the door of my room and with a smirk on my face, I replied proudly, **"Just hire a bunch of people; do the work well and get the right clients to build a successful company. There is nothing complicated in it."**

I was wrong!

That day when we were sitting in the park with ice creams in our hands, my young mind could not contemplate the things that are required to run a successful company. But now after all these years, I finally know! It is never that easy.

Building a successful company is not just about hiring people or investing money or getting clients. It is about building a relationship with the employees, giving them the freedom to work and leading them from the front.

Now when I think about the old days, it makes me laugh at my foolishness. But I also feel lucky since it gave me the opportunity to learn how to build a successful organization. Employees are always the key; if employees are not happy then a company can never achieve success. But I achieved it and I always credit my employees for that. It was not easy and I made mistakes on the way but I did it.

One day while I was surfing through my site, millions of questions were running through my mind.

But the question that had a deep impact on me was when I asked myself, **"What is the biggest challenge I faced in this journey?"**

I clearly remember, I was sipping on my mug of coffee and my wife was calling me for dinner but I could not rest until I figured out the answer.

But I just couldn't keep my family waiting for me at the dinner table.

I always prefer to have some family talks at the dinner table. But that day, the scene was different. One of my beautiful daughters was just sitting like a grumpy little princess. After asking several times, we learned that her team lost a quiz competition and her friend blamed her.

On being asked further questions, my daughter said, **"She said that she knew the answer but I still answered and we lost. I should have listened to her, Dad. It's my mistake, Dad, it's my mistake."**

And she sobbed and hugged me.

That day, I realized that it is Ego.

It will always be Ego. Ego is the enemy; the first enemy and the last. Unless we abolish our ego and become one with our employees, it is never possible to achieve true success. But does that mean there will be no difference between the employer and employee? Of course there will be a difference. But we must show them the way as leaders rather than just managing them.

Yes! Entrepreneurs ought to be the leaders. We must always guide them the right way. This is what I did not know that day so many years ago.

But now I have learned the truth. I have walked the path of an entrepreneur; I have made mistakes and I have corrected them to become what I am today.

Listen to your employees. Do not get blinded by Ego:

I have often seen people becoming a little arrogant after starting their own entrepreneurship. There are many who consider that listening to employees is something beneath them. Well, this is a mistake that you should not make.

Employees are not brainless robots. They are human beings with feelings and intelligence of their own. There are people who may have much more technical or practical knowledge than I do. So, it is always best to listen to what your employees have to say. I was once this arrogant fool who did not have time to listen to his employees.

But I changed!

One day many years ago I was in my cubicle, suddenly one of my employees entered in a rush. **"Sir, the server is getting crashed sometimes. I think we should get it checked or it will affect our clientele,"** he said to me. I was naturally very disturbed by his lack of manners. A simple employee storming into my cubicle and lecturing me about what to do was too much for me to accept.

"I know what must be done. Thank you for your concern. You may get back to your work now," I replied a little harshly.

But my egoistic mind failed to see that the simple employee understood something that I failed to contemplate. Thus, I suffered losses which I could have avoided if I had listened to my employee. Moreover, the employee who came rushing to me felt so insulted that he left my company.

I learned the lesson. I understood why it is important to listen to them.

From that day, I let go of my ego completely and I started listening to whatever my employees need to say. And I also managed to convince that employee to rejoin my company.

When you listen to your employees, you are essentially making them feel important. You are acknowledging their ideas and concepts which ultimately make you successful. Furthermore, it motivates them to work hard and improve once they understand that their opinions matter in the company.

Writer and motivational speaker **Robin S. Sharma** once said, **"Leadership is not a popularity contest; it's about leaving your ego at the door. The name of the game is to lead without a title."** So, let your ego go and become a true leader by starting to listen to your employees. Building a successful organization is not easy but it becomes a lot easier when your employees are by your side.

Let go of the reins:

I often hear people saying **"Don't give so much freedom to your employees. They will bring you down."** But the reality is completely different.

I am an entrepreneur; I am not the ringmaster of a circus. Likewise, my employees are not untamed animals. Thus, there must always be a certain degree of trust between you and your employees.

As an entrepreneur, it is my duty to see that my employees never feel detached from the company. They must never feel that I am the only person who will benefit from the well-being of the company.

I was not clear about this concept from the beginning but I learned it in the sweetest way possible. It was several years back and I had just started my company back then.

I was at a friend's party when I was reunited with one of my college acquaintances who had graduated before me. He also opened his own start-up and had made a good fortune for himself. **"How do you deal with your employees? How do you make them feel?"** he asked.

I was really startled by this question as I had no proper answer. **"I pay them well and they work for me in return. Why would I know how they feel?"** I replied foolishly.

He laughed heartily, patted my back and said, **"This is the dumbest answer I have ever received. Always treat your employees well. Do not let them feel left out of** your company. **Your employees are your biggest asset and how they feel determines how your customers feel. So, if it means giving them the certain authority to run your business, then do it. Or else you will never be successful."**

It really made me think and I understood what he was trying to say.

The party was over; I returned home and locked myself in my room. I thought over and over again.

And finally, the picture was clear.

From that day forward, I have never let my employees feel left out. I always give them the vibe that they are as crucial to the company as I am.

The result? Well, it is splendid.

I am free to do the important stuff while other things are managed by my employees. Plus, my business is running efficiently and each day we are getting closer to our organizational goals.

So, give your employees certain authorities or powers to run your company on your behalf. Never let them feel that they do not matter to your organization. And you will be able to understand the difference it makes soon enough.

Train them well and give them access to run your company:

A good leader or a great manager? What do my employees need me to be? This is probably one question that has given me sleepless nights throughout my life.

While growing as an entrepreneur, I have always found people making suggestions to me on how to manage my employees efficiently.

But I never wanted to manage them; rather, my concept was always to lead them from the front.

I wanted them to trust me.

Just like any regular day at my office, I was discussing some really important facts with my employees. One of my employees suddenly replied, **"We trust you, sir. We always have."**

Believe me, that's all I have always wanted. I wanted my employees to trust me and give me a chance to guide them.

Besides trust, I have to be their leader as well.

I needed to groom myself into a valorous leader in shining armor who can guide them in the battlefield and manage his army like a true leader.

Managing employees is important in a few fields. However, it is much more important to become a leader. A great manager gives the employees work and receive reports on progress in return. But can you consider a manager as a good leader as well? Not necessarily!

Leaders are the ones who compel people to follow them. They inspire others and induce people to join in their cause. Can managers have the same effect on employees? Well, in most cases, they don't.

So, my concept was always clear; I was meant to be the leader of my pride. I do not direct my employees to what they need to do. They know their job and they do it with utmost perfection.

My work is to inspire them to do their job efficiently. I work to help them visualize the things that we can achieve together. Moreover, I try to be the person who will always be there to help them out and listen to their problems. I don't know whether I have become a great leader but I can surely say that my approach has helped me to build a successful company.

The fact is, managing makes the relationship between the employer and employees very mechanical. Often, employees feel that they are unimportant to the company which is never good for any organization. But when you lead them, when you work with them side by side, they become an integral part of your cause.

They start to share your passion and believe in your plans. Employees feel motivated and they start to work hard to achieve the organizational goals. It's often said that: **"If your actions inspire others to dream more, learn more, do more and become more, you are a leader."**

So, this is what I always try to be!

This is something that every entrepreneur wants to achieve. But it is always necessary that you take the right approach to lead your employees. Wrong moves can seriously damage your image. And one thing that you must avoid at any cost is micromanagement.

There are people who consider micromanagement to be an important step in managing employees to fulfill their goals. However, this is an utterly bad practice. Micromanagement is the process where you closely observe and control every action of your employees. But you must never indulge in such improper practices.

Employees are not sheep neither are you a shepherd. So, you must always refrain from interfering in the work of the employees. When you start to have a say in everything that your employees do, it creates a distance between you and your employees. It drives them away from you!

Sometimes I had the urge to check on my employees but I stopped immediately.

"Abdul, you should not. Remember, you may have to pay a heavy price in future once you start practicing micromanagement. Stop, Abdul. Just stop."

Yes. I confronted and spoke to myself to stop myself from getting involved in micromanagement.

I knew that once I started with it, I couldn't stop.

You must never forget that the employees are working in your company because they believe in you and your cause. But if you narrow their actions, if you do not give them the freedom to work freely then it becomes very choking for them. Their performance degrades and you drift away from your goals.

This is something that I have seen happen in front of my eyes.

There was a man I knew who became the owner of their logistics business after his father died. At the beginning, he was very gentle and kind to the employees and the business started to grow. I was really very surprised to see how good he was at running the business.

I was mistaken!

One day I was sitting at my breakfast table and sipping my morning tea. Suddenly, a friend of mine called. He informed me that the logistics company that I thought was running very well had gone bankrupt and the owner had put up his company shares for auction. How did it come to happen? I was really baffled by the news.

Later, I learned that he was micromanaging his employees. The employees who had been working in the company since his father's time felt miserable as he completely usurped their freedom of work and managed their actions at every instance. As a result, the company which had been seeing profit went completely bankrupt.

In the words of John C. Maxwell, **"A leader is one who knows the way, goes the way, and shows the way."** So, be the leader; inspire your employees and ensure success for your company!

Motivate your employees to finish the work as soon as possible:

When you are working in a company, it is always better to get your work done as soon as possible.

Why is it so?

If you delay the work then its complexity increases and it becomes too hard to complete it efficiently. This is the exact reason I always ask my employees to get their work done as soon as they can.

Cyril Northcote Parkinson, the famous British historian and author, wrote in his book Parkinson's Law, or The Pursuit of Progress that **"Work expands so as to fill the time available for its completion."**

What does it mean? It means if you leave your work for later then it only grows in complexity and it becomes too hard for you to complete the task efficiently. Parkinson worked as a bureaucrat in his younger years, so he was well aware of the work processes in organizations, which is why Parkinson's Law is still very famous around the world.

EMPLOYEES ARE THE KEY 51

As an entrepreneur, it is always my duty to make my employees understand the importance of this concept. And I always try to compel them to use it to their advantage.

We all know people who have trouble completing their work before the deadline. Rather they favor doing the work at the penultimate moment.

Well, this is a wrong approach to doing work.
And I can guarantee this from my personal experiences. I was in college back then. Exams were approaching and I had not touched any subject. My teachers asked me to start studying as not much time was left before exams.
I did not listen.

As the exam period started, I began feeling helpless. The syllabus was huge and I did not know anything. It was too difficult for me to learn everything two weeks before the examinations. As a result, I got very poor marks.

It made me understand the value of getting work done as soon as possible. But how this concept was important for employees still was not clear to me.

But it did not take me long to understand the importance of Parkinson's Law once I started walking the path of entrepreneurship.

A few years back, I asked one of my employees to solve a customer's problem on an immediate basis. However, he was not so eager to do the work immediately. As he delayed, the problem worsened and it became too much for him to solve it later.

I lost the customer!

But I was not furious with this outcome rather I called in the employee and made him realize his fault. From that day onwards, he never delayed any work again, and he became one of the top performers.

There is nothing better than finishing your work efficiently rather than delaying it. It will help employees to become extraordinary performers. In every company, the extraordinary performers matter the most. They help you to achieve the operational efficiency that is needed to transform your small start-up into a large company.

So, let them understand the value of Time. Time is of the essence; proper time management is what matters the most ultimately. Motivate your employees to understand Parkinson's Law so that you can climb the steps of success.

Smart employees vs. hardworking employees:

Smart employees or extraordinary employees – which one does your company need most?

Well, why don't you make use of both?

Actually, a company needs both smart employees and hard workers. Smartness is important when it comes to running a business. An employee must show a certain level of smartness to deal with the customers, vendors and shareholders. Without smart employees who can easily tackle any situation, you will never be able to ensure success for your company.

However, the employees must be hard workers too. When you are trying to set up a company, you must be willing to work hard to get everything right. This trait must be present in your employees also.

I was always reminded by my mentor that it is the employees who run a company. So, if they do not have any intention to work hard then smartness alone can never help you to achieve success.

Smart people are not necessarily hard workers and every hard worker is not necessarily smart. So as an entrepreneur, you must always look for individuals who have both traits. What does that mean? It means you need to hire people who are smart as well as willing to work hard.

The famous designer **Chris Pardo** once said in an interview, **"Before you can work smart, you need to work hard."**

This has always been one of my favorite quotes as it explains the true symphony of a successful enterprise. By working smart, you can surely finish work faster and reduce work pressure by almost 20%. However, for the other 80% of the work that needs to be finished, you will have to work earnestly.

What I am trying to say here is that without hard work there is no point in being smart. These two characteristics must always co-exist in order to grow your company into a successful enterprise.

This is one concept that I grasped early in my life.

I was very close to my uncle. Well, he was more of a friend to me. Amid all the fun and pampering, he would also teach me some valuable lessons in life.

One day, we were sitting in a park when he asked me: **"Abdul, can you see that mule?"**

I said: **"Yes, Uncle."**

He smiled at me and said, **"The mule works very hard but still it gets treated badly. It means if you only work hard in your life and do not think smartly, you can never achieve success."**

I nodded! He continued: "**Now you have seen a koel bird. Don't you agree that it is a smart bird but at the same time, very lazy? Naturally, they fail to even a build a nest and raise their children. So, smartness alone cannot bring you greatness. Okay, now tell me who you need to be like.**"

I was confused. I did not know what to say.

My uncle understood my situation and said: "**Be like an ant. Ants are very smart yet they work hard persistently. That is why during the winters when others suffer due to lack of food, the ants survive and live happily!**"

I understood what he wanted to say. From that moment onwards, I have always tried to make smart decisions without compromising with hard work. And I have always trained and motivated my employees to do the same.

When they are in the office, they are using their brain to deal with the clients and get new customers. But at the same time, they are working hard to meet the organizational goals.

"**There are no shortcuts to success. Hard work is the smart work**" – this is something New York based entrepreneur **Jorah Engler** said in an interview. It is basically the truth. Unless you work hard, you will never be able to achieve success.

Thus, it is not a question of smart employees or hard-working employees rather it is about having employees who are both. Train your employees well and motivate them so that they can work earnestly and smartly.

Growing ordinary employees into extraordinary performers:

Every company needs extraordinary performers, as they create the difference between success and failure. But the question is how will you grow your employees into extraordinary performers?

If you had asked me this question 15 years ago then I would not have been able to answer.

But now I can!

There are several bad practices that employees indulge in and one of the major mistakes is multitasking. You should never encourage them to do so. When you are multitasking, your concentration is divided among everything you are doing. You are not concentrating enough on a single part of work and it reduces efficiency which in turn causes loss.

So, you must never encourage such practices by your employees. Train them to concentrate on their work and get it done quickly as well as efficiently. In this way, you will be able to maintain the work efficiency in your office.

As I have said several times, time management plays the crucial role. If you want to reach your organizational goals then you will have to utilize your time smartly and you must never encourage the wastage of time. Even though you can train your employees to work timely, there is one thing that always wastes a lot of time.

Don't you want to know what is it? Hold on tight, this can shake you off your chair a bit because it is **"company meetings."**

Oh! Don't get me wrong. Allow me to explain.

Company meetings usually stretch from 45 minutes to an hour or even longer. Explaining the agenda to your employees then explaining the solution; all the processes take so much time. And you must find a way to curtail that.

What can you do?

Well, you can make your employees aware of the meeting agenda ahead of the meeting and inform them about your plans. In this way, they will be aware of what the meeting is really about and you will be able to save the time that gets wasted explaining everything to them.

Just talk to them, interact as necessary and you will be able to wrap the meeting up within 10 minutes. It will help you to save a lot of time and encourage the employees to give their best.

Lastly, praise your employees in front of everyone as it will always motivate them to give their best performance.

Don't we love to hear when someone sings paeans of praise about us? Everyone loves to be praised. And employees are no different. Especially, when you applaud their outstanding achievements in front of a room packed with an audience.

The joy that they feel inspires them the most to get things done extraordinarily. In the words of actress **Mae West, "An ounce of performance is worth pounds of promises."** So, inspire and train your employees to grow as extraordinary performers as it will help you to achieve the impossible.

SECRET 3

An extraordinary employee does the work of ten ordinary employees. So, train them to become extraordinary!
So, what is your secret to build a successful organization?

4

HIRE SLOW AND FIRE FAST

I always thought, **"Hiring the right people is the most crucial thing for an employer."** The screening process always needs to be done very cautiously to find the best among all the applicants.

Employees are the greatest asset for every company. So, unless you are hiring the right people, you can never achieve the success that you dream of.

Don't you agree?

But one fine day, I asked myself: **"What is the secret of hiring productive employees? How should you do it?"**

I challenged myself; I trained my mind and rushed through thousands of pages for a good two years.

And now I can confidently say I can! I can identify the gem easily.

Experience is the key to choosing the right people for your enterprise. There are a plethora of tactics and strategies written in management books about recruiting employees. However, in real life, it is your instincts and experience as an entrepreneur that ultimately helps you to choose the right people.

This is what I have learned.

But how will I apply it in real life?

Well, with time I learned.

It is always better to take it slow. Do not rush while hiring an employee. Be patient, describe the job to the candidate, judge whether the candidate is fit for the role, and track performance during the training period before hiring permanently.

"What is the point in following such a long process?"

This is something that several people have asked me over the years. Well, recruiting employees is what I must do as an entrepreneur.

Now, if I hire unfit employees to my company, then they will also lower the efficiency of others through their inability to work efficiently. So, it is always better to go slowly rather than face the problem of ineffective and inefficient employees.

But what if there is an employee in your company who is unfit in every aspect? What if the employee is inefficient, lazy and has no regard for deadlines, then what should you do?

Fire that employee right away!

Appears to be a negative concept, right?

Even the "old me" thought so.

I distinctly remember one of the nightmarish situations of my life.

One of my employees was not fit for my company. But I still gave him numerous chances because I considered it inhumane to snatch someone's source of earnings. And trust me, this decision dragged me down into a situation that resulted in the loss of three of my clients and earned my company a bad reputation in the market.

The companies were big names in the global market, and it did leave a negative impact. It took me two months to gain back my business's reputation.

I had countless sleepless nights. All my focus was on regaining my lost reputation.

There were times when I was like, **"I lost it all. I destroyed my own company."**

All my confidence was lost.

And to top it all, the employee whom I thought of reconsidering time and again was adamant about not leaving my company unless I paid him a hefty compensation.

"What should I compensate him for? It's he who ruined everything, and now he dares to threaten me?"

I understood the true meaning of the proverb **"not all that shines is gold."**

When I gathered back all my confidence, I said to myself, **"It's okay to fire your employees."**

Firing is also an important concept that you need to learn. When a body part gets putrefied, it is always better to cut it out; otherwise, it will result in your demise. Thus, if there is an employee who is inefficient and has no regard for the company values then get rid of that employee.

This must be done as soon as possible. Do not delay it unnecessarily. Once you have made up your mind, just get it done with.

Your company is like a train with you being the engine and all your employees being the coaches. And everyone is linked with the couplings made up of excellent performance. If one coupling breaks, it can cause your train to derail.

Thus, never hesitate to fire an inefficient employee. You can never make everyone happy. So, get it done as soon as possible since the more time you lose, the more your company suffers.

An employer must always be ready to make the harsh decisions. I have learned this from my life experiences. No matter how hard the decision is, if it benefits your company then you must gladly make it.

Your goal to build a successful company is bigger than you or any employee. Therefore, make the right decisions always without hesitation.

Be efficient enough to recruit the right people and at the same time be strong enough to get the inefficient people out of your company.

"Don't hire for the sake of hiring. Hire because there is no other way to do what you want to do." This quote from entrepreneur **Sam Altman** describes what a responsible employer must do.

Only hire people when you have no other option. Most importantly, do not forget to give a proper job description for the position. Hire people wisely and get rid of them if they are inefficient. It is your decision that makes the difference. Thus, take your steps very cautiously to achieve success.

Define the job properly:

"**What position is that company hiring for? What do they need employees for?**" These are the questions that people generally ask each other before going for a job interview.

You must always answer these issues aptly. When you are advertising to hire new people, you must always give an accurate job description so that the candidates understand what you are looking for in your fresh recruits.

I have seen several cases where new start-ups do not provide an appropriate job description in their advertisements. This is a bad practice!

If you do not make clear what you are looking for, then people will never understand your requirements. As a result, you will never be able to hire skilled employees.

I have made the same mistakes!

I was unaware of the importance of providing a proper job description in advertisements for hiring employees in my early days. I would just let people know about the vacancy and recruitment drive.

One day, I was in my cubicle when my assistant informed me that someone had arrived for a job interview. I asked my assistant to send the candidate to my cubicle.

It was a girl!

She was fresh out of college and looking for a job. On having a conversation with her, I found out that she had come to interview for the post of customer support representative. I was sorry to hear that, as at that moment there was no vacancy in that post.

I was looking for an SEO analyst. So, I humbly told her about it and said I would give her a call if any vacancy occurred.

The whole confusion arose because I was not careful enough to give a proper job description. From that day onwards, I have always been extra careful about providing an appropriate job description while recruiting employees.

Basecamp CEO **Jason Fried** once said, "**Hiring people is like making friends. Pick good ones, and they'll enrich your life. Make bad choices, and they'll bring you down.**" And it appropriately describes your responsibility as an employer.

If you do not provide a decent job description, then job seekers will never be able to understand your requirements. It will never be possible for anyone to contemplate the things that you need a recruit to do. Thus, it will create problems and will hamper your organizational efficiency significantly.

Define the job requirements carefully, as it is the first step towards making active recruitments.

Train them well and track their performance:

"**Is an interview enough to understand the efficiency of an employee?**" a friend asked me once during our college days.

"Maybe!" was what I answered as I was not sure back then.

I was just a young man full of ambitions to become something in my life. I never cared whether an interview was enough to judge the efficiency of a recruit.

I was wrong!

You can never tell how efficient candidates are just from an interview. Of course, they might have surplus knowledge about the work they are expected to do.

But can you guarantee that they are effective performers? Can you vouch that they will always be faithful to your organizational goal and will always work hard?

You can't! No one can!

That is why it is important that you take it slow. Don't rush things; just observe them for a period of time. Then you will be able to understand the ideal thing that you need to do.

But the question is how will you observe them if you are not hiring? Well, you do not have to hire them as full-time employees, rather hire the short-listed candidates from the interview as trainees.

During the training period, train these people well and provide them with various types of assignments. Evaluate their performance. In the end, hire the individual with best performance and skills as a full-time employee.

Undoubtedly, the process is a bit lengthy. But it is better to adhere to a lengthy process rather than hire wrong people to your company.

"You can have the best strategy and the best building in the world, but if you don't have the hearts and minds of the people who work with you, none of it comes to

life." – **Renee West,** the former CEO of Luxor and Excalibur Hotels, wrote this in her book and it beautifully narrates the importance of right employees in an organization.

In all my years as an entrepreneur, I have slowly learned the importance of hiring people based on their performance. Earlier, I used to recruit people just with the interview.

But then I found out something. I discovered some of the people I have hired are not at all interested in working earnestly, and they have no regard for the company's benefit. Even though they are knowledgeable about their job, they are completely inefficient in reality.

Since then I have always taken it slow. I have judged the recruits by their performance before hiring them permanently. And it has done wonders for now I have the best employees that I could have ever asked for.

Train them well and see how much they are improving. Check how willing they are to work earnestly before you choose to hire them. A right decision can make your company successful, and a wrong one can break it completely.

Achieving organizational efficiency is the prime goal for every entrepreneur. It can only be done if you have the best employees who are willing to give the best efforts in shaping your company's future. Make sure that you are making the right decision after judging the facts accurately.

Choose team players:

"A company is like a football team. Here, all players need to play well and have good communication with each other. Only then can you win the game."

A good friend of mine once told me this. And I have tried to follow it throughout my life.

Obviously, a company is like a team, and you are its captain. But you cannot win this game alone. You need a team which will work together and will have your back always.

Teamwork is essential! **John C. Maxwell** once said, **"Teamwork makes the dream work, but a vision becomes a nightmare when the leader has a big dream and a bad team."** And it holds true for an organizational environment.

I remember spending countless hours on picking the best employees for my company. And now, my business is gaining the fruitful results.

So, you need to hire employees who are great team players. You need to choose people who will have a great rapport with their colleagues and will be able to work as a team.

However, it's hard to understand whether an employee is a team player. While hiring employees, you will find people mentioning that they are great in working with a team in their resume. But in most cases, these are false assurances.

How will you understand?

As I have mentioned earlier, the best thing to do is to hire employees after judging their performance throughout a training period.

During the training period, give them complex assignments which will require them to work in harmony with others. Check how well are they performing before coming to the final decision.

I knew it since my struggling days. There were moments when I just shut myself from any communication with my team, and later, I regretted it like many others.

Teamwork is important in every company. It builds the organizational spirit and culture. When your employees work as a team, the business goals become more important to them than their individual goals.

In return, it boosts your company's operational efficiency and helps you to achieve success.

"Why do you try to form a team? Because teamwork builds trust and trust builds speed." Russel Honore, a retired general, once said this in an interview.

And once I understood its value, I have always tried to follow this ideology.

I was sure about one thing back when I started my company, and it was to build a proper team in my business. But everything in life does not turn out the way you plan it to be.

As I hired employees and started my company, I expected them to know the value of teamwork. For the first few days, I was pleased with the results.

I was wrong!

Everything took the worst turn, and my company's interests were in danger.

I became scared for the first time!

I was in shock; I could not understand how things became so much worse. It turned out my employees had divided themselves into two groups.

Confused?

Well, let me explain the scenario in detail.

The dreamer-me, who hardly had any idea about the harsh reality, had hired two individuals who I thought were most talented of all. And these two proved to be the root of all my problems. As the work progressed, the ego clash between these two became worse, and they even stopped communicating with each other. But I suppose the breaking point of my company's work culture was other employees choosing sides. Yes, they had chosen sides among themselves.

Sounds childish? Trust me, the situation was even worse. In numerous instances, I had to stop my work just to calm down the situation.

The two groups would not cooperate at any cost.

All my company's processes were jeopardized. And at one point, I thought I would have to close my business.

It was time for me to take the necessary action.

One day, I finally decided to call all my employees (except the two self-proclaimed leaders of the two groups) for a meeting.

In spite of being the grumpy boss, I played the role of an understanding boss.

"Do you guys really value your job?"

Of course, they all answered with a big yes.

That's when I played my card and sternly said that if the problem continued, they would become jobless all too soon. They responded positively to my call and promised to work enthusiastically as a team keeping aside their individual problems. But I was not done yet as it was time for me to meet the principal culprits. Initially, I was a bit skeptical about having any interaction with them.

But then, that would have been an injustice.

All these years I have learned that we must hear both sides of the story. And so I did.

I called the two to my cubicle.

"What is the deal with you two? Why can't you two work with each other peacefully? You guys are not doing a good job for the company, and you are preventing others from working too. I can't allow this to continue. We are a team here, and your juvenile actions are hurting the team spirit of my company. Now, you choose what you want to do," I told them sternly.

But much to my dismay, they turned out to be profoundly stubborn. They refused to work or even communicate with each other. I knew what I had to do, so I didn't waste any time.

I fired them.

My company came back from the verge of closure and once again the work was efficient.

Now, the point is, you can avoid all this and hire people who value the importance of teamwork. Just track how well they work with other employees and their rapport with others before hiring them permanently.

In the words of **Andrew Carnegie, the famed** industrialist, **"Teamwork is the ability to work together toward a common vision. The ability to direct individual** accomplishments toward organizational objectives. It is the fuel that allows common people to attain uncommon results."

Don't you agree?

When your team game is on point then nothing can stop you from achieving success. Thus, be wise and test trainees well before hiring them.

Look for people who share your hunger:

Are you hungry enough for success? Do you want to make your enterprise big?

I ask myself these questions every day.

An entrepreneur must have hunger for success to a certain extent. Without this personality trait in an entrepreneur, the growth of an organization is impossible. As American business tycoon **Les Brown** said: **"Wanting something is not enough. You must hunger for it. Your motivation must be absolutely compelling in order to overcome the obstacles that will invariably come your way."**

When you crave success badly, it helps you to innovate and formulate better business strategies to achieve organizational growth. It helps you to move forward and get past all the hurdles that come your way.

Now, the thing is, your employees must share a similar attitude. They must also be famished for success.

Why is it necessary? When employees share the beliefs of their employer, it helps to form a special bond and understanding between them. It also helps them to work peacefully and cooperate with each other at every point.

Patrick Lencioni beautifully addressed the necessity of this craving: "**For organizations seriously committed to making teamwork a cultural reality, I'm convinced that 'the right people' are the ones who have three virtues in common – humility, hunger, and people smarts.**"

When an enterprise achieves this kind of peaceful relationship among the entrepreneur and employees, its work efficiency increases manifold and achieving the goal no longer remains impossible. At this point, every single employee works toward organizational success by overlooking their personal motives.

So, as an entrepreneur, it is your duty to establish this kind of understanding with your employees. But in order to achieve that, you need to hire people who believe in your hunger for success.

To be honest, before I became an entrepreneur, if I ever had a complete disagreement with my boss over how to work on a particular project, I would have just done the work for the sake of achieving it. The main reasons for lack of interest are a conflict in work styles and a difference in organizational goals.

If I being the boss of a company can agree on disagreement of interest, then I should also try and find the perfect remedy.

So the next step is, how will you understand whether someone truly shares your beliefs? To help you understand this, I will have to take you again to the very basics of hiring employees.

As I have emphasized, the training period is the key to judge the efficiency as well as the personality traits of potential new hires. However, these character traits are interwoven with the effectiveness of the employees.

People who crave success always try to give their best. They implement new strategies and techniques of dealing with their work. And every day, they work hard to outshine themselves. It is as if they are continuously fighting a war with themselves. Every day they are working hard to become far better than the day before so that they can achieve what they seek.

Thus, the employees that have a similar hunger are always the ones who work earnestly as well as smartly. During the training period, you will be able to understand how the recruit works. You can analyze whether the individual is working hard and taking quick actions to benefit your company by tracking performance.

In the end, if you are satisfied with the results then hire the individual as a permanent employee of your organization.

Personally, I have always tried to stick to this method for hiring employees for my organization. And it has always provided me with great results.

This is one concept that I grasped very early in my career and all thanks to the wisdom of my mentor.

"Always surround yourself with the people who share your beliefs and fiery will. Employ the individuals who have the same craving for success as you. If you can do that then you will never have to look back," one day my friend/mentor told me over a cup of coffee.

Surprisingly, it has always been a great motivator for me. Now, after so many years, I still walk on the path my mentor showed me to move forward to achieve things that once I thought were impossible to achieve.

Are you ready too?

"Concentration comes out of a combination of confidence and hunger." Arnold Palmer, a legendary American golf pro, said this a long time ago. And it is still true. If your employees have the hunger, then they will always find a way to concentrate on achieving success.

Get rid of dangerous elements ASAP:

"What happens if you keep a rotten apple along with the fresh ones?" my mother once asked me as a child.

I could not answer!

Yeah, it's obvious for a 5-year-old kid not to understand any philosophical statement.

So smartly I went on to reply, **"It will just stay rotten, and when you will notice it, you are just going to throw it away. The fresh ones will be safe."**

My mother smiled at me. She asked me to sit with her and said: **"It also damages the fresh apples."**

I still remember how surprised I was. It was something new that I had heard. So, I could not control my amazement.

"Get rid of all the harmful elements from your life while you can. No matter who they are, never hesitate to cut them away. Otherwise, they will always prevent you from achieving success. They will never allow you to move forward," my mom advised.

Now, when I think about it carefully, I can understand that my mother gave me the most valuable piece of advice that day. Most importantly, this advice holds true for every instance of your life.

HIRE SLOW AND FIRE FAST

A bit of advice that every entrepreneur needs.

No matter how efficient your workforce is, there will always be one or two people who will hamper the organizational effectiveness of your company through their inappropriate actions.

If you look carefully, then you will find that these individuals are not efficient workers themselves. But they manipulate others, create chaos and prevent their colleagues from working efficiently.

Honestly, it is a serious problem for any start-up or a small company. In such an organization, you cannot allow anything to disrupt the work flow and operational efficiency. Continuation of inefficient practices can spell doom for your enterprise.

Trust me, there is no return.

What do you need to do then? If there are inefficient individuals among your employees, then do not hesitate to get rid of them to keep your workforce efficient and sincere. Do not wait any further after you have got the indication, fire these bad elements as soon as possible.

There is no problem in hiring employees slowly. But when you find out that there are people in your company who are not willing to work properly and are incompetent in all aspects, then do not waste any time to fire them.

Though it may look harsh, always remember that the interests of any one individual cannot be bigger than those of the company. As an entrepreneur, you must not be driven by emotion, rather you must deal with every situation logically.

You need to think what the probable outcome will be if you take action and then you will have to act immediately.

I have learned this from my own experience. I was not always a follower of the "fire fast" concept. I was too lenient, and some people used to take advantage of my leniency.

At that time, I had an employee who was truly worthless from every aspect. He was highly talented, there was no doubt of that. But he never had the zeal to work hard.

He was more interested in creating mayhem within the company by creating problems among other employees. I had known about his actions but was too scared to respond appropriately. I didn't want to lose a talented employee.

It was clearly a mistake.

The business processes of my company were being affected badly and thus it resulted in low efficiency.

One day while talking with a friend (who is a successful entrepreneur himself) I mentioned this problem and asked for an honest suggestion.

He was the one who helped me to understand the concept of "fire fast."

"Never be lenient with these things. If you know who the problem is, get rid of him as soon as you can," my friend suggested.

So, I fired that employee the very next day.

Surprisingly, it improved work efficiency greatly and my enterprise was back on the track of success. s

In the words of author **Michael Bassey Johnson: "No matter how valuable you are and your ideas, fools will certainly play both of you down, so exclude yourselves**

from the inflammatory environs of fools." Never tolerate any foul element in your company. Don't be fool enough to commit a mistake like mine.

Anyone who disrupts the workflow within your organization is a threat, and it is always better to get rid of such people as soon as possible.

So, fire fast and hire only efficient people, as this is the only way to achieve success.

SECRET 4

*An exclusive training period to judge
the efficiency and performance of recruits
is the wisest thing that you can do to hire people.*
So, what methods are you following to hire employees?

5

STAFF CONFLICTS: A GREAT ENEMY OF YOUR COMPANY'S WORK CULTURE

"**Never let the ego build up. Let go of it. It will make your life much easier.**" A chapter in my values education class quoted these lines, and it's never too late to understand their meaning.

Years have passed since that day, but the words are still etched in my mind. I could not comprehend the true meaning at first.

But with time, everything was clear.

Ego is the root of all evils. It prevents you from moving forward and becomes the reason for your downfall. Mainly, it creates problems among friends or colleagues and destroys a harmonious relationship. Be it a family or company, ego destroys all bonds single-handedly.

In any organization, the efficiency of the employees determines the success of the company. If they work well with each other and have a great understanding of themselves, then nothing can stop the business from achieving success.

However, it runs both ways. If the employees are not compatible with each other; if there is no teamwork and a conflict exists between them, then it can become fatal for your business.

As I have said before, in most cases, ego problems give rise to conflict among employees. Ego clashes in the workplace are a common thing, but when it takes the shape of full-fledged conflict, then it becomes inevitable for you to take necessary actions to save your company.

Blame ego, employee nature or anything else, conflict among employees can turn your business into a war front. The problem is even if the friction is between two individuals, it can have a significant effect on the efficiency and productivity of your company.

However, it is still true that conflict is not always a bad thing, as it can give rise to healthy competition between two employees. It can motivate them to work hard to outdo each other.

But that is not always the case! It may not be essential to get rid of some employee conflicts.

Well, conflict seems to be a bad idea but for some purposes it acts as an advantage.

Entrepreneurship comes with several challenges. Dealing with staff and solving the conflicts is a challenge to every entrepreneur. And if you want to achieve success then this is something that you need to do efficiently.

You are the leader of your company. So, you can always motivate your employees to let go of their ego and other problems to work in harmony.

Yes, you can inspire them, train them and make them understand the value of teamwork in an organizational environment. With your leadership, you can shape the different individuals into an efficient workforce.

"A good manager doesn't try to eliminate conflict; he tries to keep it from wasting the energies of his people. If you're the boss and your people fight you openly when they think that you are wrong – that's healthy." This particular quote coming from actor and director **Robert Townsend** has often inspired me.

What the employees need to understand is that the interest of the company is much more important than individual interests. The company is much bigger than any one person. It is your duty to put this concept into their brains.

When the employees start putting the company ahead of everything else, only then can they resolve the conflicts among themselves and work together for the best interests of the enterprise.

How to deal with employees who do not get along?

"No sir, I can't work with him anymore. He is terrible."

Being the boss of the company, I get to hear this kind of complaint often. If you follow the words of inspirational writer **Shannon L. Alder, "The most important thing in communication is hearing what isn't being said. The art of reading between the lines is a lifelong quest of the wise,"** you will actually understand what it takes to be an employer, the head of the company.

Managing employees is a complicated affair itself, and it becomes much more complex when you have to deal with people who do not even acknowledge each other.

"Intervene at the right time. Go to the root of the problem. Understand what are the reasons behind the cold war and solve it from the roots for good," said my mentor once while addressing the issue.

I have always tried to live by his words.

Of course, it is necessary for you to intervene at the right time, before the conflict takes an ugly turn. Remember that you are not dealing with two kids who fought. The concern is much graver and if you do not intervene at the right moment, it can very well destroy the work culture of your company.

It is true that you can always fire an employee if things get too ugly but that is not always a solution. Your company can never run successfully if you keep on firing people. Thus, it is essential that you take the right action at the right time.

Furthermore, you need to understand the factors which are causing the problem. You cannot just force two warring employees to shake hands and forget everything. It will never work. So, understanding the problem is highly critical.

I tried to force two employees of mine into a healthy relationship, but I failed.

One beautiful morning I saw both of them eagerly waiting for me, even before office hours.

"What's up? What's wrong with you guys?" I proceeded to initiate the chat.

"I just can't work with him anymore," said employee number one.

"And neither can I," said the other employee.

This took place within a week of the forceful reconciliation.

I knew that the idea failed terribly.

So, how would I do it? How would I understand the reason behind the conflict and resolve it?

The best way to do so is to talk with the employees separately. See things from their point of view. The thing is, you don't have to force them to like each other.

Two people can work together even if they are not fond of each other. The goal is to get them at least to acknowledge each other's presence and work as a team to help your company to become successful.

Once you have identified the problem, you can encourage them to solve it. You can formulate unique exercises for them to understand each other in a better way to get rid of their problems. With constant encouragement from your end and team-building activities, they will likely move past their problems to work efficiently with each other.

This is a problem that all entrepreneurs face at some point in their careers.

As I have mentioned, I already faced it.

Let me give a more detailed insight into the story.

A few years back, I found out that my employees were not working as efficiently as they should. A strange uneasiness was reigning in my office. There was an uncanny silence among the employees. It was an indication of a storm to come!

Luckily, I intervened at the right time, so I was able to avert the hurricane, tornado or whatever was coming to my office. I called one of the employees to my cubicle and asked:

"What is the deal with you guys? You are not working properly. And there is a strange atmosphere in the office. What's wrong with you folks?"

I found out something grave!

I discovered two of my employees had ideological differences which had turned into an ego fight, and they were unwilling to work with each other at any cost. And that was the whole reason behind the inefficiency of the employees and uncanny ambiance in the office.

Both of these warring employees were efficient workers. They were brilliant and had helped the company to accomplish several feats in the past. So, it was a problem. When two of your key players refuse to work with each other, it affects your company significantly.

You already know that I tried to reconcile them forcefully and it did not work out.

So, my next plan was to call them individually to my office.

"Yes, now explain to me what's wrong between you two?"

I talked to them and tried to understand what the problem was. Both of them had lots to complain about each other.

Once I understood what the problem was, I devised my plan accordingly. I made them know that they were both right in their own stance and asked them to see the situation from each other's point of view.

While figuring out the solution, I always recalled the quote from **Dale Carnegie** that states, **"When dealing with people, remember you are not dealing with creatures of logic, but creatures of emotion."**

As a result, it helped them to understand their mistakes and they agreed to work with each other. The problem was eventually solved and my company was restored to its former glory once again.

The point I am trying to make here is that you are an entrepreneur, not a parent of two quarreling kids. So, you will have to be intuitive and intelligent enough to deal with any situation. Encourage them to get past their problems and solve the conflict efficiently.

Understanding co-worker conflicts:

"**The more we run from conflict, the more it masters us; the more we try to avoid it, the more it controls us; the less we fear conflict, the less it confuses us; the less we deny our differences, the less they divide us.**" – **David Augsburger,** professor of pastoral care

There is one thing you need to understand – leadership and conflict are like two sides of the same coin. Thus, they always go hand-in-hand. And you need to address the dispute at the right time. If you are scared or unwilling to solve the problem, then you must never be in a leadership role.

Entrepreneurship is a demanding task and understanding as well as addressing conflicts is an important part of it.

Employees spend so much time with each other in the office. Their colleagues become more like their family members. If you think carefully then you will understand that the employees spend more time with each other than with their family and friends.

So, they often form strong bonds with their colleagues. However, it is also true that this proximity can give rise to nasty fights and conflicts among the employees, which can result in the loss of work culture in your company.

Workplace conflicts are inevitable, and there is no way to avert them.

Yes, this is one of those things that will happen at some point in time. There is nothing you can do to prevent it from ever happening. Though you cannot avoid the co-worker conflicts, you can surely address the situation and put a full stop to it efficiently.

The best way to deal with the conflict among your employees is to deal with it.

"How many people have doomed their company by not addressing the conflicts? Who has ever achieved success by refusing to take necessary actions?" an old friend once asked me these questions while talking over the issue.

I know the answers now.

No one! No one has ever been able to escape the fire of conflict. So, never try to avoid it; rather stand tall and face it head-on.

It is essential for every entrepreneur to have the ability to identify a conflict, understand its nature, find the causes and take quick action to get rid of it. Only then will you be able to become a real leader, otherwise it can turn out to be the reason for your greatest failure.

Speaking of understanding co-worker conflicts, how do you think you can do that? How will you understand the nature of the conflict and the reason that is causing it?

Well, it is easy enough to figure out if you know where to look. The most common reason for conflicts among employees is their emotions. There are a group of people in every organization who use emotions to manipulate people. These people are not such efficient workers.

And if you look closely then you will find that they lack the essential substance that is required to become an efficient performer. Rather they use their manipulative nature to control others' views and opinions about themselves.

If something does not go as planned or they fail to do something, such employees will start new drama within an organization to create chaos and conflict. Ultimately, it leads to the downfall of your organization.

"Every conflict we face in life is rich with positive and negative potential. It can be a source of inspiration, enlightenment, learning, transformation, and growth – or rage, fear, shame, entrapment, and resistance. The choice is not up to our opponents, but to us, and our willingness to face and work through them." These words of conflict resolution specialists **Kenneth Cloke** and **Joan Goldsmith** are truly on point.

Thus, the first thing you need to do to understand the conflict is to identify this band of people. But how will you know which ones are manipulating other employees to create conflict in your company?

The answer is pretty simple. You will have to establish proper communication with your employees. Only by communicating effectively with your employees can you identify these people who are causing the conflict.

It is always better to talk with employees individually and listen to what they have to say. Yes, listening is an essential part as it is the only way you will be able to understand the reasons behind the employee conflict. And once you have identified the culprits, take just action to end the dispute for good.

Now that I have told you how to understand and deal with a conflict, let me tell you something that you must never do. Obviously, you must never let yourself be driven by emotions.

Making important decisions on the basis of emotions is never a sign of a real entrepreneur. Thus, you need to use your emotional intelligence in this case. Once you have identified the culprit, you will have to take steps intelligently to deal with the problem.

To do so, you will have to ask yourself a question.

"What will I get from it?"

Yes, before taking any action you will have to ask yourself this question. It will help you to take the right step which will benefit you most.

So, be intelligent. Identify the problem and deal with it intelligently, so that the conflict ends and your company achieves the success that you are looking for.

Make time for employee relations:

As I go further into discussing effective ways of solving employee conflict, it is essential for you to understand that having good employee relations reduces greatly the chances of employee conflict.

Sometimes inspiration and knowledge come from completely unexpected sources. And these instances are too divine to ignore. Once I was traveling by train when I had the chance to get acquainted with the HR manager of a multinational company. I was young and was about to start my organization. So, we were having fun talking about important business-related things.

"Do you know which essential thing must exist in a company?" asked the stranger.

"You tell me," I replied with a hearty smile.

"The most important thing in any organizational setup is employee relations. The dynamic between the employer and employee decides the fate of a company. Thus, no matter what you do, always try to have excellent employee relations," the stranger explained.

With every passing day, I understand how vital his advice was. That's why I always try to stay true to it.

I always try to have a great dynamic with my employees. Plus, I take care of them and look out for their problems to help them work without any hindrance.

"Employees are the greatest asset for any organization"– this is a phrase we all are familiar with. However, only a handful of companies actually treat their employees as their biggest asset.

Why is it necessary to have a great relationship with employees?

The relationship that you have with your employees determines how engaged they are towards the company. A relationship formed on the pillars of distrust, fear and lack of respect makes the foundation of your business weak and makes the employees disengaged.

But it can be averted. With proper communication and using other ways to improve the relationship with employees, you can quickly avoid such outcomes.

However, there is something I need to talk about before moving forward to the ways of establishing a proper employee relationship.

What are employee relations?

I have been talking about it for quite some time. But what is it actually? How can we define it?

According to the management textbooks:

"Employee relations or industrial relations is a term used to define the physical, emotional, practical and contractual relationship among any employer and the employees in an organizational setup."

Actually, when it signifies a relationship in between an entrepreneur and an employee which is forged from mutual respect, trust, transparency and appreciation for each other, then this is constructive employee relations. And this is something every company aims for.

On the other hand, a relationship formed from lack of transparency, from fear or from disrespect often gives rise to friction or conflict among employees and the organization.

Every entrepreneur tries to prevent the latter from happening as it often demotivates employees from giving their best.

But how will you do it? How will you keep a positive relationship with your employees?

Essentially, there are a few steps involved in it. The first and foremost thing is to have excellent communication with your employees.

Author **David Goodman** nicely explained the concept: **"There is a psychological law that says: Appreciate, and you prosper; belittle and you lose. Unless we learn to apply this law, as psychological as it is spiritual, we're doomed to an existence of mediocrity, frustration, and defeat. Appreciation is no simple, vague theme. Appreciation is a real force. It is governed by a principle almost as direct as a law of physics: We draw to ourselves the good of everything we appreciate."**

Communication is always the key to motivate your employees as well as to have great relationships with them. The very first step of having great communication with your employees is to assure them that you are always there to listen to their problems.

Hassles of daily work are enough to demotivate anyone. But if employees know that there is someone who will listen to their problems and try to solve them, it is actually a great relief. Then you can give them advice and help them out which will establish a positive relationship with your employees.

Another thing that you can do to establish a great relationship with your employees is to provide them with the recognition that they deserve.

As we have discussed before, every person craves attention. Thus, when you recognize their good work and praise them in front of everyone, it charges them up. You not only establish a healthy relationship with your employees but you also take the motivation of your employees to the highest point.

"Good job, buddy. You are actually living up to my expectations."

Once I said these words to one of my employees, and it boosted his efficiency.

He was one of the employees whose efforts always went unnoticed.

Honestly, I crave appreciation and so does everyone. I really couldn't stop feeling guilty. Being the boss of a small business, it's not impossible for me to appreciate the hard work of all my dedicated employees.

Once I realized that fact, there was no looking back. I promised myself to keep appreciating all the deserving employees because they are my real jewels.

Finally, there are a couple of things that you must not do to have excellent employee relations. The very first thing that you must never do is micromanage the employees. Some people consider it to be beneficial.

But let me tell you that it is a lie. Micromanaging the employees can never bring anything good to your organization, rather it rubs your staff the wrong way. You ultimately lose the respect and trust of your employees. And once the trust is lost there is no way that you can regain it.

Secondly, you must never have favorites among your staff members. Of course, employees differ from each other in skills, performance and efficiency. But it doesn't imply that you must have favorites among them.

An entrepreneur is always like a father figure to employees. So, if you start picking favorites then you will soon lose the respect and trust of other employees.

Ultimately, it will become the reason for your downfall. Thus, treat all your employees equally with compassion and care to establish a stable employee relationship.

In my case, I have always tried hard to have a great relationship with my employees. As of today, I have a great relationship with my employees.

My employees know that no matter what I will always be there to listen to their problems and to help them out.

Furthermore, I always track their performance and provide them with feedback and gifts, a bonus or a raise to recognize their extraordinary performance. Plus, I always make them feel important; I always get them to realize that they are as important to the company as I am. It undoubtedly boosts our relationship and motivates them to do efficient work.

Employee relations are perhaps one of the essential things in a company. So, you need to give your all to establish a positive relationship with your employees.

Be wise and take necessary actions to build a great relationship with your employees. If you can successfully do that then you will be able to reduce the conflicts drastically.

Resolving staff conflict: The effective ways:

Now that I have given you some idea of employee disputes, it is time to find the ways to put a stop to them permanently.

Conflicts are common in any organization. However, it can really disrupt the workflow of your entire organization if you allow it to fester without taking the necessary actions. So, you need to tackle it head-on rather than avoiding it.

But one thing is sure; managing these conflicts can be tricky. Especially it becomes tricky for a start-up entrepreneur who does not have any previous experience of dealing with employees.

In a workplace, there will always be a group of people who will play a dirty game by manipulating others to cover up their lack of performance. This is something you already know.
But you must act wisely so that you can end the conflict without sowing the seeds of a bigger problem.

Being an entrepreneur is not enough to end conflicts. You will have to become a true leader to do so. A leader is a person whose responsible actions earn respect from employees. Leadership is not a concept rather it is a way of bringing out the full potential out of the employees.

An important part of developing the full potential of the employees is to get a clear idea of what the conflict is about from them as quickly as possible. Then you can act swiftly to put an end to the conflict.

Healthy competition among the employees to perform well is always necessary. However, when it transforms into utter chaos and mayhem, then it can do more harm than good. Thus, it is important for you to use your leadership instincts to seize the perfect opportunity to solve a problem.

Now, the question is how you will do it? How will you put a stop to the conflict? Well, there are a few ways to do it efficiently.

Once you have understood the nature of the conflict, you will have to wait for the perfect opportunity to act. You cannot sit down and pretend everything is good as you and I both know that will worsen the situation. So, wait for the perfect opportunity to act swiftly to end the conflict permanently.

I am stressing perfect timing so much because once it gets out of your hands, then you will not be able to contain it.

This brings us to the second point of solving a conflict. You must know your boundaries. You must understand when a conflict is solvable and when it is out of your hands. Once you have a fair idea about that then you can easily perfect your timing to take the required action.

You need to carefully observe and understand how the conflict is progressing through your company. With vigilant observations, you will always be able to understand when it is the right time for you to act.

But there is still another thing that you need to understand. What will be the perfect plan of action for you?

You cannot just use your position to force your employees to solve the problem. It will not help. Rather you will have to understand their differences and you will have to see things from their point of view.

When you start seeing things from their point of view, your plan of action will be completely clear to you. And you will be able to act accordingly to get rid of the problem and restore your company to its full glory.

In all these years of being an entrepreneur, I have faced employee conflicts but I have always been able to get rid of these conflicts efficiently.

I had just started my company back then and I was going with full speed to establish it. But destiny had other plans for me perhaps and my business started to fall drastically.

I felt helpless.

I investigated the matter and found out that a few of the new employees who recently joined my company were not working with each other in a proper way which was ultimately causing the loss to my business.

I knew that I had to act quickly; I could not just ignore the situation since it may end my tenure as an entrepreneur completely. So, I organized a joint meeting with all of my employees.

"What's wrong with you people? Can I get a good explanation?"

While they proceeded, I listened to them carefully. Ego clash was the reason for the employees to go on a full-scale war with each.

The respective employees had their own opinion on solving a particular problem and as they could not find common ground, it created the ego clash which in turn gave rise to the conflict.

So, I carefully tried to observe the situation from the point of view of all the responsible employees. Since I couldn't just impose my point of view on them, I tried something different. I analyzed the ideas and formulated a common one by taking the best parts from each. My employees accepted it readily and it put an end to the conflict permanently.

The most important factor in solving a conflict is your leadership qualities. The way you analyze the reason for conflict and act makes the ultimate difference.

Remember, as life coach and author **Vironika Tugaleva** said, "**In some ways, we will always be different. In other ways, we will always be the same. There is always room** to disagree and blame, just as there is always room to take a new perspective and empathize. Understanding is a choice."

Thus, be wise and communicative if you are truly trying to solve a conflict. Once you are able to do that, you will be able to solve any conflict irrespective of how dire the situation is.

SECRET 5

When it becomes impossible for you to deal with the manipulators who create the conflicts in the company, fire them ASAP. It will solve the problem.

So, what are you doing to solve the staff conflicts?

6

WORRY IN BUSINESS AND HOW TO HANDLE IT

Sir John Lubbock, a renowned British scientist and polymath, once said, **"A day of worry is more exhausting than a week of work."** That's a harsh reality of human life.

Worries are something that all entrepreneurs need to deal with. In all these years of entrepreneurship, I have found that there will always be something that will have me worried.

But is there any way to get rid of it?

Of course there is! And I am going to tell you all about it.

Worrying is never an option if you want to become an achiever. It de-motivates us and brings fatigue. Above all, it reduces our productivity greatly which only creates more worries for us.

But how can you stop worrying?

It seems impossible. Isn't it?

Obviously, it seems to be the hardest thing in the world but it is not impossible. Actually, if you know the tricks, it is pretty easy to strip yourself of all the worries.

As far as I can recall, my first encounter with worry was probably during a mathematics test. Now, like most other people, I was not too fond of math. All those formulas and calculations were too heavy for my brain to handle. Thus, I would get worried and that resulted in bad grades. The situation continued until my father told me something vital. Yes, he gave me my very first lesson on how to deal with worries.

Only a few weeks were left before exams and I had sunk myself deep into the books. However, my arch-nemesis mathematics was strong too. Even after studying for hours, trigonometry or calculus was still not under my grasp. I freaked out!

I lay on my bed battle-worn and tired. My father had a knack of watching over me while I was studying whenever he would be at home. As I lost the battle and lay on the bed with fatigue, he sat beside me and stroked gently through my hair.

He affectionately said, **"What's the matter, son? Why are you lying on the bed at this hour?"**

"Dad, I will probably fail in mathematics. I cannot remember any equation. I feel lost and tired! What should I do?" I asked without looking at him.

"Stop worrying first. You worry too much and that is causing all the problems," my father replied.

I was baffled and could not understand what he was trying to say. So, I looked at him with a surprised look on my face.

"Worrying about something will never help you in any way. Instead, try to go deeper. Understand where you are

lacking and how you can solve this problem. Only then will you be able to control this weakness," my dad said.

Well, that was terrific advice and after so many years, it still helps me to win over worry. It is always better to ask yourself the necessary questions.

Ask yourself, **"How, what, why, where and when?"** Analyze the answer and be rational about any problem rather than spending countless hours worrying over it. Worry brings depression and anxiety which in turn decreases your work efficiency and increases fatigue. So, shut the door on worry and see new opportunities opening before your eyes.

Working habits to prevent fatigue and worry:

Drawing your attention towards what my father said, let me give you a short piece of advice to help you understand. The simplest advice that I can give is to work hard without thinking about the result. And you need to question yourself always before reaching the conclusion.

However, that is merely the head and tail of it. In order to understand how to prevent worry, we must venture deep to unearth its causes.

I have already explained to you that worrying is a bad thing to do and it can very well become the reason for your downfall. But what leads to the rise of worry?

Through my experience in life, I can say that confusion and doubt give rise to worry. If you are confused and have a mind full of doubts, then you will eventually get worried. Most of the people in this world try to tackle a problem or situation without having proper knowledge about it. This gives birth to confusion and doubts. Thus, the vicious cycle of worry and fatigue starts.

As I have already explained to you about the relationship between worry and confusion, now it is time to decipher the secret of getting rid of all the worries. It is a four-step process and absolute precision is required at every step in order to succeed in the others.

After reading many books and talking with several intelligent people, I have now understood what these four steps are. But it amazes me every time I think back to that forlorn afternoon when I received that crucial advice from my father. He was right! Every word he said was true.

What is the first thing that you need to do to get rid of worry?

"**Collect the facts objectively and impartially,**" my mentor said. "**I always try to collect the facts from others' points of view. I do not try to feed my ego or try to collect only the facts which will prove my opinion on a matter is correct. But I try to collect them completely impartially, so that they can lead me in the right direction.**"

Will this help to evaporate all your worries?

Of course it will. As I have stated earlier, the lack of knowledge creates confusion which in turn gives rise to worry. Collecting the facts will provide you with knowledge which in turn will help you to clear your confusion and get rid of worry.

However, there is a tiny problem in it. The facts will have to be impartial and objective.

Why so?

Let us take the words of author and speaker **Sean Covey** to better understand the matter: "**Seeing things from a different point of view can help us understand why**

other people act the way they do. We too often judge people without having all the facts."

This is one way to look at the problem. When human beings hunt for the facts, they often become fixated on finding the ones that will bring them personal satisfaction. But that is not the right way to deal with it. You must be able to see things from different points of view so that you can understand where the problem is and acquire true knowledge.

For this particular reason, I pretend that I am collecting the facts for someone else. It helps me to achieve clarity and see things from others' point of view. Furthermore, when I am trying to analyze a problem that has become the reason for my worry, I act like a detective looking for evidence at a crime scene. It helps me to gather the information which in any other condition would have escaped my sight.

With this we took the first step towards preventing worry, but what next? What do you need to do once you have collected the facts?

It is time for interpreting and analyzing the facts.

I have already told you about the importance of asking yourself questions in the form of **"what, why, how, where and when."** And that is exactly what analyzing the facts is all about.

Analyzing the facts provides you with a clear picture of the problem and helps you to understand what to do in order to get rid of it. We all know about the great American inventor Thomas Alva Edison. Edison was a great thinker and he had an interesting method of dealing with worry. Edison had several notebooks which he used to jot down all the facts, and he put different points of views in separate columns. Then there were pages where he would write questions which he would answer honestly. This helped him to understand the problem and come up with a good solution.

All I am asking you to do is to follow the same method since it is something that actually works.

Let me relate an incident that happened with me. A few months earlier, our rate of hosting renewal from customers suddenly dropped. I could not find any plausible reason to explain this sudden change in behavior. Naturally, it had me worried. But worrying was never an option for me. So, I opened Microsoft Word on my laptop and typed:

Why am I worried?
My company is facing sudden loss.

What has resulted in this sudden change?
The rate of renewal of the hosting package by existing customers has decreased by 25%.

Why did this happen?
Our hosting packages are not offering enough when compared to that of the competitors for the same price.

What do I need to do?
Revise the hosting packages and make our offerings much better than our competitors'.

This is actually a part of the conversation I had with myself that day on MS Word. Since I had the facts, when I asked myself the questions the best possible result presented itself automatically in front of me and my worries evaporated immediately.

In the words of American actor and motivational speaker, **Mr T: "I don't worry. I don't doubt. I'm daring. I'm a rebel."** So, do not waste time worrying; analyze and interpret the facts to formulate a solution.

Speaking of formulating a solution, it is the third step in preventing worry. Formulating a solution is not as easy as it may sound; you have to be very rational and wise while doing it.

I already told you about the conversation that I had with myself regarding my worries due to the loss that my company was facing. After analyzing the facts, I concluded that upgrading our packages was the right thing to do. But this was a mere hypothetical conclusion that I came up with.

Formulating a way to upgrade our packages was not as easy as it may sound and I knew that very well. **"What should I do? I cannot just reduce the price; it will make a bad impression among the customers. I cannot just increase my offerings without increasing the price. It will further reduce my profit margin,"** I thought.

After running a simulation in my mind of all the data I had and the steps that I could take, the solution presented itself. As soon as the solution was ready, it was time to take the fourth step to drive the worry away finally.

The fourth step is always the easiest step since all you need to do is adhere to your decision. Thus, I implemented the solution by creating new offers as well as discounts for existing customers on hosting renewal. As a result, the rate of renewal saw a steep increase again. Hence, the battle against worry was won!

The first U.S. president, **George Washington,** said, **"Worry is the interest paid by those who borrow trouble."** As I have stated several times before, worrying does not bring anything good. It makes you fatigued, anxious and above all a failure.

So, do not waste your time worrying about anything. Be rational about a problem and try to solve it with your intelligence rather than emotions. Study the problem and understand the situation to collect the facts impartially. Then analyze and interpret the facts, come up with a solution and finally implement it to have your worries flee permanently.

One evening many years ago, I asked my mentor, **"How do you make all your decisions? How do you keep so calm and cool all the time?"**

"Abdul, you still have a long way to go. But you will eventually learn too. In all these years, I have found that thinking about a problem beyond a certain point always creates confusion and doubts. So, if you can control your thoughts then the confusion will never arise and you will never have to deal with worry in the first place," he replied with a smile.

Still, it is not always possible to control your thoughts. So, if you are experiencing worry, use the four-step method to get rid of it completely.

Adding one hour a day to waking life:

Why am I writing about fatigue when this chapter is all about worries?

The thing is, worry and fatigue are interrelated. Worry often gives rise to fatigue whereas fatigue can become the reason for your worry.

Fatigue has a vivid effect on your mental as well as physical health. If you consult a doctor, you will be told that fatigue makes you vulnerable to diseases and several other physical problems.

On the other hand, a psychiatrist will tell you that fatigue makes you susceptible to worry and depression. Either way, it reduces your work efficiency, something which is highly important in the life of an entrepreneur. In other words, if you prevent fatigue, you will also be preventing worry.

"Prevent fatigue to prevent worry," this is just a mere summary of it. Clinical psychology explains the phenomenon in a more detailed way. It has been found in several clinical studies that proper relaxation is the key to preventing fatigue which in turn keeps the worry at arm's length.

Dr. Edmund Jacobson, the former director of the University of Chicago laboratory for clinical psychology, dedicated his life to studying the effectiveness of relaxation as a method for treating several conditions. According to him, **"Any negative emotional state or nervousness cannot coexist with complete relaxation."** In other words, we human beings cannot continue to worry if we are relaxed.

To make it simple for you, I have found two easy rules for you to follow. Firstly, rest whenever you get the chance. And secondly, rest before you feel tired.

Why do you need to follow these rules?

Even though I would love to take the credit for developing these rules, the credit goes to the U.S. Army. Soldiers must be physically as well as mentally strong. That means they must not be fatigued and they should prevent themselves from getting worried.

Thus, army trainers after doing extensive research came up with these rules and today they are followed worldwide. You will often find soldiers throwing down their packs and resting for a few minutes every hour in order to replenish their energy even though they are not that tired. It helps them to withstand all situations without fatigue and worries.

When I am on business trips, meeting the vendors, having important conferences and attending important meetings, it usually leaves me completely fatigued if I do not rest well. And if I do not rest well then it leaves me completely tired and it increases my anxiety as well as worry.

I cannot let it continue otherwise it will hamper my work. That is why I remain in bed till 9-10 a.m. and make important phone calls as well as video conferences. Then I attend the meetings or visit the places that are in my schedule. And upon returning to the hotel, I rest again for an hour or two to keep myself recharged.

It helps me to carry out all my work without any pressure and to prevent worry completely. Yes, I prevent worry completely. I prevent worry because I rest frequently whenever I get time.

"How do you remain so fresh and cheerful all the time? You are one of the most hard-working guys I know. Don't you get tired? And how do you deal with the stress and worries of business?" a vendor of mine once asked me.

"There is no secret to it. I rest often and keep myself fresh. That does the trick," I replied.

I am telling you the same thing. There are no other secrets to it. Just take few minutes' break every hour to rest for a bit and that will help you to prevent fatigue as well as worry completely.

It's not just the army, if you turn the history pages then you will also find that every great leader or personality used to rest frequently to keep the worry at bay.

Relaxation is the only therapy that you can follow to get rid of fatigue and worry. Follow your heart. Take a rest before you feel tired and you will be able to add one hour a day to your waking life.

What makes you tired and what can you do about it?

Noted author **Dale Carnegie** said, "**Our fatigue is often caused not by work, but by worry, frustration and resentment.**" Of course, it is one of the harshest truths that you will ever come across.

I have already told you how fatigue and worry are interrelated. But till now I have only discussed how fatigue gives rise to worry. However, it goes the other way too. Worry can give rise to fatigue.

Does that not sound very convincing?

Well, you are not alone. The reason behind tiredness and fatigue baffled the experts too for several decades. Our brain can work for 12-15 hours without any rest and it is a completely tireless and efficient worker.

Then what does make us tired?

J.A. Hadfield, one of the pioneers in psychiatry in the UK, wrote in his book, "**The greater part of fatigue from which we suffer is of mental origin; in fact, exhaustion of pure physical origin is very rare.**"

Being one of the most renowned psychiatrists of his time, Hadfield unveiled the secret behind the fatigue that we witness.

Yes, it is our mental stress and worries that make us fatigued. The tiredness that arises from hard work can be easily handled with a good amount of relaxation.

What will you do about the fatigue that has a mental origin?

It is a proven fact now that hypertension, worry and emotional upsets can result in fatigue. However, you cannot take up any conventional way to deal with it.

Is there no way to deal with it?

Of course there is!

Ease up and let your muscles rest. Save energy and it will help you to get rid of the worries.

But what created these worries or tensions in the first place? It is the general notion of hard work that can be identified as the culprit.

In my life, I have heard people saying, **"If you do not feel the hard work from within your mind, then you are not working hard enough."** This creates the problem in the first place.

I am working on something with all my dedication but it does not mean that I will have to take the unnecessary stress.

Most of us feel the hard work by worrying about it and taking on stress. As a result, we often scowl, hunch up and tense every muscle in our body to prove that we are working hard. Where does that lead us? It creates tension and makes us stressed and worried which in turn gives rise to fatigue. Most people hate wasting money, but they do not realize that they are wasting so much energy in following the common notion of hard work.

Let's now concentrate on how to deal with fatigue that arises from worry and stress. Well, the best way to get rid of stress is to fool your body and mind.

Wait, what do I mean by fooling your mind?

We are the master of all our senses and feelings. So, the best way to get rid of worry and fatigue is to make your mind understand that there is nothing to worry about.

Yes, this is something that I follow personally. No matter how proficient I am in dealing with stress and worry, it is impossible for me to prevent fatigue completely. So, how do I deal with it? Let me tell you that story.

Often when I get tired due to work stress or worry, the muscles between my eyes become fatigued. They get strained which causes pain.

But if I give in to the tiredness then I will never be able to complete my work. So, what do I do? I have a secret mantra for it.

I sit relaxed on my couch, close my eyes and chant my mantra. In my mind, I say, **"Let go. Do not frown. Relax. Let go."**

Do you think I am talking nonsense?

I am not!

It is the truth. Practice it and you will be able to get rid of fatigue significantly.

From where do we start relaxing our body? Is it our mind or nerves?

Actually, the relaxation of our body starts from our muscles. We relax our muscles first, then the mind and nerves get relaxed automatically.

So if you are feeling fatigue and stress, chant the mantra and you will be able to get rid of this fatigue easily.

How to eliminate 50% of your business worries:

Wouldn't it be great to have our worries reduced by 50%?

Of course it would be!

But is it plausible? Yes, it is and there is no inherent joke in it.

Every entrepreneur faces business worry and it torments us verily. So, it is a dream of all entrepreneurs to have their worries reduced by half.

Even though it seems impossible, it can be done easily. And I am going to show you how.

According to famous psychiatrist **Dr. Alexis Carrel, "Businessmen who do not know how to fight worry die young."** Since worry is that serious, let me show you how to reduce more than 50% of your worries without wasting any time.

I can tell you how based on my own experience. Earlier in my career, I used to spend most of my business days in solving the problems of my employees. I had to attend meetings every day to solve the problems that my company was facing.

Usually, all these meetings had a general routine. My employees would recite their problems to me and at the end they would ask, **"Sir, how will we solve this problem?"**

The process would literally increase my tension and worry. I knew that I had to deal with this problem in some way. So, I made some rules.

Firstly, I forbade them from reciting their problems and asking me for the solution. Secondly, I told them to jot down a few questions on paper and answer them. After answering the questions, they can ask me for help.

So, what are those questions that I asked them to write?

What is the problem?
What caused the problem?
How many ways can the problem be solved?
Which is the best way to solve the problem?

After I made these rules, my employees stopped coming to me so much because they were able to find the correct solution to the problem.

Incidentally, it also reduced more than 60% of my worries. And I was able to breathe a sigh of relief.

For every entrepreneur, the biggest worries are caused while solving problems of employees. The stress that is caused while thinking of all the ways to solve every problem that a company faces really shortens our life.

But if employees are able to solve their own problems then there will never arise a situation where you will have to face that kind of worry. And you will be able to lengthen your life.

Worries are constant in our lives but we can get rid of them completely. We can surely find ways to prevent worry from tormenting us. Be smart and wise, take every step logically and then you will be able to lead a much more worry-free life.

SECRET 6

Do not let anything confuse you. Know your facts and analyze them perfectly to prevent worrying.
So, what will you do to get rid of your business worries?

7

STRUCTURE YOUR BUSINESS TO RUN ITSELF

"What should young entrepreneurs want from the business? What should be their big goal?" a reporter asked a business leader.

"Well, they must want a business that can run itself. So that they can go on vacations without being noticed," replied the business leader with a smile.

A business that can run itself is the thing that every business leader wants today.

But why is it so? Why do you need a business that can go on even in your absence?

There may be a time when you need to attend to something other than your business. Or there can arise a situation which can compel you to step out for a few days.

What will happen then if your business cannot run itself?

By my guess, it will sink deep into the ocean of failure. But that is not desired. I am an entrepreneur too; so I understand very well how painful it is to even think of your business falling apart. Thus, it is always important that you provide your business with the ability to run without your help.

But this whole concept sounds a bit weird. Does it not? You have built your company; you are responsible for all the success that your company has witnessed.

Why would you ever want to get yourself out of that equation? Why would you want to remove yourself from the daily operations of your business?

Maybe you do not like them as much as you think. As the leader of your business, if you are deeply involved in the daily functionalities, then at some point you will feel the strain that it puts on you. You will not have time to do anything else or go on vacations. Above all, this dependability will turn out to be the reason for the failure of your business.

Now that I have made my point, it is time to shift our focus to making the impossible possible.

Yes, structuring your business in such a way that it can run itself may sound like a farce. But it is not unachievable! If you have the right strategy and the determination, then you can turn it into reality.

But firstly, I want to make something clear to you.

Even though we are aiming for a business that can run itself, it does not imply that you will have no responsibilities.

As the entrepreneur or the prime leadership, you will always have your responsibilities. Our goal here is to structure your business in such a way that it can run without trouble even if you need to take a break for a certain period of time.

The idea of structuring my business so that it can run in my absence hit me years back. As I was just starting at that time, I used to plan all the operations of my business and there was no scope for automation. But I was too foolish to understand that it was a bane for my company.

One day I was driving from DBS Business Centre to the Income Tax Centre in Shivaji Nagar, India. So, I turned right from Balkundi Circle to Queen's Road. Suddenly a little girl ran in front of my car out of nowhere to pick up her doll.

I did not know what to do but I had to save her. So, I steered left. My car hit the side rails and darkness laid its blanket over my eyes.

I had an accident.

I regained my senses in the hospital. And found out I had a slight concussion, a broken right arm and a fractured leg. Not to mention the shock I was in after regaining consciousness.

I had to go through a long and strict recovery process. I was stuck in my home for three long months.

I asked my doctor a few weeks after returning from the hospital: **"Can I please go to my office? I am worried how my business is running without me."**

The doctor looked at me as if I had demanded one of his kidneys and said: **"You are lucky to be alive. Now, do you want to be in bed for your whole life? Don't be a kid; everything is fine in your office."**

Everything was not fine!

My business was in a shambles. Revenues were down; the old customers were leaving and there were hardly any new customers. It was another shock for me and I was completely devastated.

I turned to my mentor for help. He listened to my problems and said: **"Do you know why your business is facing such a disaster now? It was depending entirely on you. We are all humans, Abdul, and these situations can arise every now and then. You cannot escape this fact. There is no doubt that your business will recover. But is that your ultimate goal? What if you need to take a break for a few months at some point in the future? Do you have any plan to prevent your business from becoming a fiasco then?"**

No! I didn't have any plans to keep my company from such a disaster. Thus, I was helpless. I turned to my mentor and said: **"Help me out, please!"**

"Hey, there is nothing to be depressed about. Cheer up! There is a way and I am going to tell it to you. Structure your business in such a way that it can run itself. Make your business independent. That way you will never have to worry about your business even if you take off for a few months," my mentor said with a smile.

The idea filled me with positive energy and I knew what I had to do. So, I used all my newfound energy to make my business independent. As of today, I can proudly say that my business is independent. I do not need to be involved in everything as it can run on its own without any trouble.

"The first rule of any technology used in a business is that automation applied to an efficient operation will

magnify the efficiency. The second is that automation applied to an inefficient operation will magnify the inefficiency," this is somethingMicrosoft's **Bill Gates** said a long time ago. But it will never run out of significance. You need to take every step very carefully to ensure that your business runs efficiently without any hassle when you are not physically or mentally present to devote yourself to it. And I am going to show you how to achieve it.

Simplify your business operations:

Focusing on what Bill Gates said, you will have to keep the efficiency of your business operations constant in order to successfully structure your business in such a way that it can run all by itself. However, a great hurdle that stands in your way is the complexity of business operations that accompany business growth.

I do not think it is unknown to any entrepreneur that with growth in business, complexities in operations also increase exponentially. The increase in complexities of your business occurs naturally with time. It is not your fault or the fault of your employees. As a business grows, the processes and operations become diverse which in turn gives rise to the complexity.

But why am I asking you to simplify operations?

The answer is very simple.

You cannot hope for your business to run itself if the operations are highly complex. Actually, a business can run all by itself only when the employees become capable of carrying out all the business processes without any help from the leader.

However, complexity can break this rhythm. It becomes too confusing and tough for the staff to do everything if the tasks are highly complex in the first place. Even though business growth is accompanied by complexity, if you do not do what is needed, then the growth of your business gets easily outpaced by the growing complexity.

So, what do you need to do?

I think you know the answer already. You will have to take the necessary actions to simplify the processes. Drawing your attention to the suggestions that my mentor gave, let me tell you how I simplified my business processes.

"Simplify the roles and responsibilities of your employees. Do not put too much pressure on anyone. Distribute the responsibilities equally among your staff and explain their individual roles to them clearly," suggested my mentor.

I called in my employees and defined their individual roles as clearly as possible. Miraculously, their efficiency increased manifold and I was able to sense it within a few days.

The next thing I was told: **"Do not set long-term goals. Rather go for more impactful 90-day priorities for your business. Most importantly, track the weekly performance of your business carefully."**

I did what I was asked and I could feel the change immediately. My employees were not clueless anymore and they had their definite part to play. Above all, the efficiency of my business had increased manifold and I was one step closer to providing the desired structure to my business.

"Dealing with complexity is an inefficient and unnecessary waste of time, attention and mental energy. There is never any justification for things beincomplex when they could be simple," Edward de Bono, a well-known British psychologist, said this decades ago and this actually what I am trying to tell you.

Dealing with complexity reduces the working efficiency of your employees which in turn prevents your company from growing. So, get rid of the complexity at the very beginning. Simplify the processes by defining the roles of your employees clearly; set short-term 90-day goals for your business to achieve and track the progress on a weekly basis.

Why will it help you? Well, your employees will have a clear idea of what they need to do and with the short-term goals, you will be able to track the progress of your business much more efficiently. Most importantly, your business will be able to run all by itself if you take a break for days.

Famous singer **Tony Bennett** once said, "**My whole premise has been, right from the beginning that it would take me a lifetime to learn to explain myself as an artist. As you grow older, you learn what to do and what to leave out. You kind of simplify your work and get the same thing done with fewer strokes. It's pretty interesting to me.**" And if you think clearly, this exactly the thing that we all are striving for.

Do not run away from delegating:

"**The inability to delegate is one of the biggest problems I see with managers at all levels,**" said **Eli Broad** to a reporter. A long time ago Broad, an American business tycoon, said this in an interview. The moment I read it, I found it very interesting and I knew this was something I would need to be extra cautious about when I became an entrepreneur.
But I failed miserably!

I have already told you about the loss that my business faced when I met with an accident. But why did my company face such a calamity? There were efficient employees who could have managed the company on my behalf; but why did they fail? They failed because I failed to delegate. I failed in the thing that I always considered to be necessary to run a successful company.

Later, my mentor made me realize my mistake. Actually, what I was doing was not correct.

It was basically not enough. I was still taking all the pressure on myself rather than dividing the pressure among my staff members. This was the mistake that had cost me most. I had to again rebuild my business from shambles.

But there is no way that you will have to witness the same fate.

Remember the mantra, **"Delegate the work to reduce the losses."**

It is a very common trait even among the top entrepreneurs to do everything by themselves.

"If I do this myself then it will be done perfectly. I will be able to do it more efficiently than others," we all think like this at some point in our career. But it actually shows your immaturity. No, you are not the only one who can do all the work efficiently and it is never advisable to take all the pressure on yourself.

You will have to put your faith in your staff and you need to delegate the work. Only by doing this can you increase the operational efficiency of your enterprise.

When you try to do everything, then you are basically holding back your company from reaching its full potential. Furthermore, you are helping the complexity to increase. As I have stated earlier, rising complexity in business outpaces growth. Thus, it prevents your company from achieving the organizational goals.

It also has another side effect. Since you are trying hard to do everything all by yourself, you are making yourself non-expendable and everything becomes dependent on you. So, if anything happens which compels you to take a leave from your company, everything starts to fall apart and your business becomes a big fat mess.

Is that acceptable? Is it what you are striving for? Is that what your goal is? Definitely not! Thus, you need a proper plan of action to delegate the responsibilities among your employees in order to elevate your business processes.

How will you do it? This is actually very easy to achieve if you know what you are doing. You need to put your faith in your staff. I am going to show you how.

"Identify the low-priority responsibilities and start delegating them at once. See how well your employees fulfill these responsibilities so that you can safely provide them with high-priority responsibilities," my mentor told me when I asked him what I needed to do.

Yes, you will have to entrust your employees with the responsibilities so that they can fulfil their duties and take your business ahead. But if you are too weary to take this essential step then you will never be able to achieve what you seek. Most importantly, you will never be able to structure your business in such a way that it can run all by itself.

"Don't be a bottleneck. If a matter is not a decision for the president or you, delegate it. Force responsibility down and out. Find problem areas, add structure and delegate. The pressure is to do the reverse. Resist it." American politician and former defense secretary **Donald Rumsfeld** once said this in a conference and he essentially spoke the truth.

It is always more complicated to do the opposite of delegating responsibilities and this extra pressure becomes the reason for your downfall. Your employees are a part of your family and you need to put your faith in them. So, delegate the responsibilities and take the necessary steps towards making your business able to run all by itself.

Predict the outcomes and take necessary actions:

I do not know anything about predicting the future but predicting business outcomes is totally possible. Actually, it is all about calculations. No, I am not talking about probabilities and favorable outcomes. I am talking about predicting the outcomes of every step that your company takes.

Here, you need to understand one thing: that the maximum limit of making these predictions is 90 days. Anything beyond that is considered to be the vision or goal of the company.

Now, getting back to predicting the outcomes; as I said earlier, it is something that needs to be calculated. There are no shortcuts and obviously, the position of the stars will not be of any help in this case.

You are already familiar with market research. It is an essential part of business. Predicting outcomes is basically the market research which you do to understand the path that your business will follow.

Whenever my company launches a new offer, my team does all the necessary calculations to understand the flow of my business. Actually, my team considers market trends, customer behaviors and other necessary variables to predict the path that my company will follow in the next 90 days.

But why is this necessary?

I met a professor from the Indian Institute of Management Ahmedabad on one of my trips and I asked him the same questions among many others.

"We all know that the business world is full of uncertainties and we do not know what will happen in the very next moment. However, if we have a clear graph of what the trend of the business will be over a certain period of time then we will be easily able to take the necessary actions to prevent the business from any immediate danger. If you have all the variables then it is pretty easy to plot the curve and predict the outcomes," replied the professor.

So you can clearly see the necessity of making predictions.

Now it is time to understand how predictions are related to structuring your business in a way that it can run all by itself.

There is nothing complicated in this answer. If your company has a team which is able to clearly predict the outcomes then your employees will always have a proper plan of action in front of them.

Even if you are not able to carry out your duties, it will not affect your business since your business will always have a proper path to follow.

"Markets work best when there's lots of information available and a historical track record to go on; they excel at predicting things like horse races, election outcomes, and box-office results." – James Surowiecki. This American financial journalist spoke the truth. So, encourage and train your team to predict outcomes as it determines how well your business will be able to run without you.

Reward competence and promote healthy competition:

"Employee loyalty begins with employer loyalty. Your employees should know that if they do the job they were hired to do with a reasonable amount of competence and efficiency, you will support them," **Harvey Mackay**, one of the finest CEOs in the USA, said this in one of his speeches.

You already know about employee motivation as well as employee loyalty and why they are necessary for a business from the previous chapters. I have also talked about competence and how to leverage profits from healthy competition among your employees.

But what you do not know is that competition is also important when it comes to structuring your business so that it can run on its own.

Obviously, you are having questions as it sounds completely absurd.

How is this even possible? How can competition among your employees help your business to run on its own?

Healthy competition among employees always acts as a catalyst. Yes, it always acts as a motivator and compels your employees to work hard as well as earnestly to outperform others. If they also understand that their performance is being tracked and there is a chance to be rewarded if they can perform well, then they will always work hard to excel.

It is human psychology. We all like to be acknowledged and recognized for our work. If someone praises us a little then it can really boost our morale and motivate us to work hard. This is something that I experienced early in my life.

It was the time when I passed my tenth standard and got admitted in eleventh. As I took admission in the eleventh standard, my father got me into the tuition classes.

Out of all the teachers, my math teacher had the most impact on my life. I was never that bad at mathematics. As I mentioned before, I had one problem. I used to get very nervous before the exams which always prevented me from getting the marks that I truly deserved.

But that changed completely as I stepped forward to my tuition class. The teacher was very friendly and encouraging. But above all, he used to praise me every time I solved a difficult problem. He would praise me in front of everyone which filled me with the zeal to outperform others by getting the highest marks in the examinations.

So, I did! It made me realize that with a little recognition and praise, we can even achieve the impossible. We can overcome all the hurdles and achieve things that are beyond our imagination.

"Competition and competitive rhetoric can be healthy. It's what drove the United States to pursue the Soviet Union into space, creating countless innovations along the way." This is something **Wendy Kopp**, the CEO of Teach For All, said in a conference.

The progress that the USA made during the cold war era in terms of technology and innovations shows the importance of competence and healthy competition. And it must be present within every company. The competition among the employees helps your business to grow and as all the employees work hard to be rewarded, the complexity of the operations decreases rapidly.

But how does it help in structuring your company in such a way that it can run all by itself? I am getting to that part now.

I have already said that the most important thing in this equation is the employees. You do not make your company processes automatic magically with the help of any technology or software. Rather, it is the efficient performance of your employees which determines the structuring of your business.

Just stop for a moment and rewind everything that we have discussed since the start of this chapter. Firstly, I asked you to simplify your business operations. In the next step, I advised you to delegate responsibilities. I showed you the boost in efficiency that can be obtained by distributing responsibilities. Lastly, I showed you the importance of business predictions especially in terms of structuring your business in a way that it can run all by itself. Up till this point, everything is clear.

Now think, are any of these steps possible without your employees? Can your business achieve the desired structure without the help of your staff members?

Perhaps not!

If your employees do not play their part then it is absolutely impossible to get through any of these steps. They need to work hard and carry out their responsibilities in a perfect manner to ensure that your business runs perfectly even in your absence.

As we all know, the best way to get your staff to play their part is to motivate them. And if you look closely, then you will understand there are no better ways than healthy competition and rewards for competence to motivate your employees.

Encourage competition in your company and reward your employees with bonuses, promotions or gifts when they perform well as this is the only way to achieve what you seek. **"No human being will work hard at anything unless they believe that they are working for competence," William Glasser,** a well-known American psychologist, said this back in the late 1950s. After almost 60 years, every word from this quote is still highly relevant. Therefore, reward competence and encourage healthy competition as it is the only way to make this structure work.

Human life is really uncertain and you can come across a situation like mine where you may have to take a break from your business for a certain amount of time. But you cannot allow your business to be a fiasco if you are not there to lead it from the front.

Follow the guidelines and structure your business in such a way that it can really run on its own.

SECRET 7

Delegate responsibilities carefully to the efficient workers, otherwise it can create problems for your enterprise.
How do you plan to automate your business process?

8

MAINTAIN RECORDS, INVEST IN TECHNOLOGY, AND IMPLEMENT WORK CULTURE

"Did you ask your boss for the casual leave next week? Your brother is getting married next week; you need to be at home," a wife asked her husband.

"Yes, I did! At first, I thought he won't allow me CL since we are starting a new project next week. But to my surprise he approved my CL and sent his best wishes for the marriage," the husband replied happily.

Every employee has a personal life and commitments, just like us.

That is something we entrepreneurs should never forget. It is our duty to ensure that they get what they want when needed. We must make sure to provide a proper work-life balance and invest in the best technologies available to ensure that the balance does not get disturbed.

Above all, it is the duty of a leader to implement proper work culture in the company. Irrespective of what your company size is, there should be an appropriate work culture. Without work culture, it is impossible for you to take your company's operational efficiency to the highest degree.

The first thing that every entrepreneur should understand is what employees want.

I have always said that employees are the biggest asset for any company. So, it is your duty as an entrepreneur to take care of your employees. Of course, a company has to be customer oriented. But if you fail to satisfy your employees, then you will never be able to satisfy your customers.

So, what do employees want?

Firstly, they want to have the liberty of taking off from work. Every employee must have casual leave. No matter what the reason is, an employee may need casual leave for family matters. Furthermore, it is essential that you provide them with documentation so that they can get hired in another organization if they deem it necessary. In India, for example, you need to provide proper certificates of employment.

Yes, it is essential that you retain your employees. But that should be done by providing them with facilities, opportunities and bonuses; something that I have talked about before.

If you are planning to hold your employees captive without providing them with a valid certificate of employment or other documentation, that is a bad idea. It will not help your business as employees will never give their best if they are forced to do the work against their will.

Secondly, you must ensure that your business is using the best technologies available in the market.

MAINTAIN RECORDS, INVEST IN TECHNOLOGY, AND IMPLEMENT WORK CULTURE

Why am I stressing this point? Well, modern technology can reduce the pressure of work on the employees to a great extent. It can help them to make better decisions and increase their efficiency greatly.

Most importantly, it will help them to maintain a proper work-life balance; something that almost every organization tries to provide their employees these days. By ensuring proper work-life balance, you will not only increase the employee retention rate but you will also encourage them to work harder with much more energy.

Lastly, there should be a proper work culture and provision for holidays. No matter how big or small an organization is, it is essential that there exists an appropriate work culture. It helps your employees to focus better on keeping up the good work without holding any resentment against the management.

Celebrate important holidays and festivals in the office; keep your office closed during festivals or on national holidays. Above all, establish a precise set of guidelines regarding everything for your employees to follow in the office and you will witness the difference it makes within few days.

These are three of the most important things that you need to remember while running a company. Back when I started my company, I was not aware of these things. Over the years, as my experience increased, everything started to become very clear to me.

"Most people chase success at work, thinking that will make them happy. The truth is that happiness at work will make you successful." This something the famed motivational speaker **Alexander Kjerulf** said in a TED talk. So, it is your duty to ensure that you provide happiness to your employees. You will have to make sure that your employees love their work and they do it happily without any resentment.

Once you can ensure that, then there will be nothing that can stop you from achieving success.

Take care of the nitty gritty: Maintain detailed staff records:

Let us now discuss another important thing that you need to do to run your company. I shed a little light on this earlier and so now, let's go on with the details. As I have stated earlier, you must provide your employees with leave if they really need it. They have their families too which they need to support; so it is essential that you understand and respect that. I shared that incident from my childhood to help you better understand the psychology of your employees.

However, it is also unwise to provide too much leave to your employees. In a company, everything must be done systematically and this is no exception. But how will you do it? How will you keep a record of the leaves that your staff members are taking and have perfect order in your company?

Well, the answer is simple. It can be done by keeping a proper staff record or a service book for every employee. The service book or staff record will have all the information about the employees no matter how small that information is. From the number of casual leaves that they are taking to the increase in their pay scale, everything must be clearly included in the service book.

Now, returning to the matter of casual leaves, you must fix a certain limit for the casual leave days that an employee can take. Yes, you need to determine a proper limit for the leaves since it is extremely unwise to give them leaves whenever they want.

In every organization, there are specific numbers of days which the employees can use as their casual leaves apart from company holidays.

MAINTAIN RECORDS, INVEST IN TECHNOLOGY, AND IMPLEMENT WORK CULTURE

But what is the big idea behind it? When an employee takes some days off using CL, no money is deducted from their paycheck. They just use up the number of days from the allotted casual leave by the company during that particular year. However, if they exceed the limit of allotted CL then it becomes unpaid leave. The amount of salary for the days the employee remains absent will be deducted from the total payroll. And this is the difference between paid and casual leave.

As I said earlier, you cannot provide your staff with infinite CLs since it will harm your company in the end. So, the idea of casual leave and paid leave was developed to maintain an order about it. After exceeding the limit of casual leave, if employees still choose to remain absent, then it will be at their own loss. The company will not bear the expenses for the actions of the employee.

This is the exact reason why it is so important to maintain a proper record.

Only with the help of a complete record will you be able to understand the number of CLs that your staff members are taking and establish a proper order. You must also create a company calendar with the fixed number of office holidays listed on it. This will provide your employees with correct knowledge about the number of holidays that they get in a year.

But there is another criterion that needs to be included in your records and that goes by the name of sick leave.

Your staff members are human beings and they can fall sick too. So, it would be non-humanitarian to consider those leaves as casual leaves. Hence, you must also determine and allot a certain number of sick days for your employees. In that way, they will remain loyal to the organization and do their work happily.

Lastly, it is very important to maintain proper certification of employment for every employee.

Every human being searches for a better opportunity and everyone wants to be big in their lives. This is one thing that we cannot deny. There may come a time when an employee may want to leave your company for a better opportunity. It is important to retain employees but it is also important to respect their wishes.

So, you must maintain proper certification of employment or other documentation for your employees. Employees can submit their certification of employment to get hired in another organization. It is important that you provide them with the certificate whenever they want. You cannot retain your employees forcefully by denying them their essential rights. Hence, maintain the certificate as it is the right thing to do.

In my career, I have had several experiences that illustrate this advice. So, I am sharing such an experience with you to make things more clear.

One day I was sitting in my cubicle when one of my staff members entered. He was pale and looking very fragile.

"Are you okay? You don't seem well to me," I asked.

"Sir, can I take the day off tomorrow? I have a high fever. As I have no CLs left, I had to come. But it is becoming impossible for me to work," he replied.

He was not lying. He was really sick and I could tell it by looking at his face.

"Hey, there is nothing to worry about. Take a day or two off if you want to. It will be counted as sick leave. Go home and take good care of yourself first," I ordered.

The employee was relieved. After that, he became one of the most earnest workers in my office as he understood that I would always be there to look after them. Hence, it is important that you always ensure that your employees do the work happily rather than by force.

Maintain the records and provide them with appropriate leaves as it is one of the best ways to ensure their complete loyalty to your business.

"I like to live life and not work every second of the day and spend time with my family and stuff like that. Balance is very important for me," the producer **Greg Kurstin** said in an interview. Obviously, you need to keep this in mind. Provide a proper balance by allowing the employees leaves and holidays. Only in this way will you be able to achieve success.

Invest in technology to improve your employee productivity:

In the world today, technology is developing at a rapid rate. Modern technologies have made the world a better place and our lives have become much easier.

Neither you nor I can deny that fact.

Every sector is depending largely on modern technologies to move forward. Then why won't you invest to implement the latest technologies in your business? With the help of technology, you will not only be able to increase the company's operational efficiency, but you will also increase the productivity and individual efficiency of your employees.

"Modern technology has become a total phenomenon for civilization, the defining force of a new social order in which efficiency is no longer an option but a necessity imposed on all human activity." This is something that French philosopher **Jacques Ellul** said back in the past and it is becoming more and more relevant with each passing day.

Yes, we all strive for efficiency. We all want to be highly efficient. We want to reach the peak of success for which being efficient is essential. Thus, efficiency is something that we need to achieve these days. Well, it can be easily achieved with the help of modern technology.

The success of an organization depends largely on the efficiency of its employees. If your employees are not productive enough, if they are inefficient, then it is never possible for you to achieve the success that you aim for. Though it is true that you can hire only efficient individuals and train them to increase their efficiency further, it does not always serve the purpose. It does not ensure that your employees will become highly productive.

The only way you have to ensure utmost productivity for your employees is to implement the latest technologies in your business.

The first purpose that technology serves is to provide access to all the available information. With the development of the internet, it has become very easy to get access to any information you want at any time. And that is the first thing that you can provide your employees with the help of modern technology.

Before the internet, employees had to maintain files to store information. It was tiring to search the files in the archives to find the required information. These things are completely absurd in modern days. And if you are still following this old system, then your company needs an immediate change.

Create a company database in your company's own server or in the cloud interface. There you will be able to store all the necessary information without any hassle.

What is the best part about this? Well, your employees will be able to access any information they want and whenever they want without draining all their energy. They will not have to

MAINTAIN RECORDS, INVEST IN TECHNOLOGY, AND IMPLEMENT WORK CULTURE

go through heaps of files, just a few clicks on the computer screen and the required data will be in their grasp.

It will not only reduce the work for your employees but it will also relieve unnecessary stress. Above all, your staff will become much more productive since they will not lose any time on searching for information. They will be able to get whatever they are looking for instantly and use it to your company's own advantage.

With the development of digital technology, the term BYOD has become highly popular. BYOD is the abbreviated form of "Bring Your Own Device." Trust me; it is really changing the industry sector greatly. The BYOD strategy is making employees much more efficient and increasing their individual productivity greatly.

But what do I mean by BYOD? Most importantly, why is it so important? The thing is nowadays we all own a laptop or a smartphone. As a result, we are more comfortable working on our own device than other devices. This is the idea that gave rise to BYOD.

Establish WiFi connection in your office so that your employees can connect their devices to the WiFi network and carry their work efficiently from their comfort zone. Irrespective of where they are, if they have their own device then they can easily continue their work without any hassle.

However, the best thing that modern technology has done for businesses is perhaps the development of ERP and CRM software suites.

And what are ERP and CRM?

Well, Enterprise Resource Planning and Customer Relationship Management are two of the most important aspects of every company. With the help of proper ERP, you can understand needs of your customers, where your business is lacking and what you can do to improve your business. At the same time, CRM helps you to establish and manage a healthy relationship with your customers.

However, it is too hard and time consuming for your employees to do the market research and analyze the data to formulate a proper plan of action for your company.

That is where ERP and business automation software come in. ERP and business automation software do all the heavy lifting for your company. They analyze the data, create a proper plan of action and guide employees with appropriate directives that they need to follow.

And the added benefit? It saves a lot of time and helps your employees to do their work efficiently. Thus, it makes your staff much more productive.

Similarly, the CRM software takes customer relationship management to the next level.

CRM software generally comes with chat support, automatic ticket generation and several other facilities. Thus, if your employees are connected with a CRM software suite, then they can always efficiently help the customers. No matter where your employees are, if they are connected to the internet, the employees will usually be able to solve the problems of the customers. Thus, it will strengthen the bonds between your customers and the company; ultimately it will pave your way to success.

This is why investing in technology is important. Technology does not just improve the work life of the staff, rather it boosts their efficiency and makes them much more productive. This increased productivity helps your business to break barriers and reach the top in almost no time.

MAINTAIN RECORDS, INVEST IN TECHNOLOGY, AND IMPLEMENT WORK CULTURE

When I started my company, I was solely depending on the individual skills of my employees rather than on the technologies available. It did not turn out really well. My business was losing to competitors and I was going far away from my goals.

"Implement the latest software suites available in your system and make a good use of the technologies available. Do as I say and you will witness the change in few days," a friend of mine said.

Well, I can't say that I fully believed in what he said but still, I invested in technologies available. I installed ERP and business automation software along with a CRM suite in my company's system.

The results surprised me greatly!

I could feel that my employees had suddenly become highly efficient and productive. Moreover, they found new energy in carrying out their work.

My business was back on track out of nowhere and it became one of the top competitors to companies which once I had idolized. So, the advice that my friend gave me that day really saved my company and career.

I am doing the same for you. I am asking you to get rid of traditional and time-consuming methods to become more tech savvy. Like me, you will also be able to see the difference investing in technology makes.

"The key thing is to invest in the future, and what that means is – when you're deploying technology or you're a technology business – is to make sure that you're keeping on the innovation cycle, where you're both creating and adopting the new business practices and the new techniques in order to drive your business the right way."

This is something that business tycoon **Reid Hoffman** once said and it is completely true. Invest in technology, keep up the good work and try to innovate since these are all the things that you will need to take your company forward in the right direction.

Implement holidays/work culture like the big boys:

Now we have reached the last key thing that you will need to run a company efficiently. Work culture is something that is most important for every organization. Without the presence of a proper work culture, it is not possible for a company to achieve success. It is your duty as an entrepreneur to implement a proper work culture in your company.

A proper work culture helps the employees to work effectively. It creates unsaid guidelines that the employees follow. Well, let me give you an example to help you better understand.

During the early days of my career, I used to arrive at the office pretty late. After some days, I noticed that my employees were not punctual. They would come to the office whenever they wanted without caring about the fixed office hours. I understood that it needed to be changed. So, instead of warning employees, I started arriving at the office by 7:30 a.m. And it worked miraculously! My employees also started to arrive within the specified time and since that day, I rarely find any latecomer in my office.

Why did this happen?

With me taking the initiative of coming to the office at the right time, I started a proper culture that was previously absent. As a result, it persuaded my staff to follow the work culture that I initiated.

MAINTAIN RECORDS, INVEST IN TECHNOLOGY, AND IMPLEMENT WORK CULTURE

However, establishing a proper work culture does not just mean finding ways to persuade employees to work efficiently. It includes celebrating important holidays and festivals in the office, arranging office parties after your company has achieved any new milestone and giving proper holidays to your staff. There should be no difference between a big conglomerate and a small company on this particular point.

I always do try to arrange little fun sessions during every festive season. To keep the festive vibe, I just ask my team to decorate their cubicles and make some food arrangement for all those special days.

Now, you might ask: How do I benefit from this?

Well, do you like to have the image of a grumpy boss? Definitely not.

Having fun with your second family, your employees, shows that you truly do consider them to be your own.
And is it harmful to take some time out and dedicate a few hours out from work for fun time? It boosts the morale of both the employer and the employee.

Including these things within your work culture will help your employees to forge stronger bonds with the company and among themselves. Ultimately, it will help you to achieve the success that you crave.

Understand these three important steps and follow them earnestly, and you will never have to regret anything in your journey as an entrepreneur.

SECRET 8

Implement new technologies and encourage innovation. Your company's productivity will increase automatically.
So, what are you doing to make your business successful?

9

WATCH THE NUMBERS AND PAY YOUR TAXES

"Have you paid your taxes?" one friend asked another.

"Of course, I have paid my taxes in advance," the other friend replied.

"Well, when are you going to file your returns?" the first friend asked again.

After a brief pause, the other friend asked: "Is it very crucial?"

This is a very common scenario in that we witness around the world when two grown people talk about income taxes and filing their returns. Most people do not have a clear idea about the things to do regarding the payment of taxes and filing of returns.

By now, you have learned from this book what you need to make your business successful. But let me break something to you. Accounting, paying taxes and filing returns are three crucial things for any entrepreneur to maintain the successful run of your business.

But before we get on with the hows and whats of this topic, let me tell you an interesting story. What is the point of this story? Well, it will act as a memorandum for you on why it is very unwise to be casual with accounting, paying taxes and filing returns if you are a business owner.

The story is about a formidable businessman who happens to be one of my respected friends. So, it has always acted as a motivation for me to be careful about these things when it comes to my company.

My friend has a product-based company which is known for manufacturing different types of products. In his early days as an entrepreneur, he had a very happy-go-lucky attitude. The products that his company sold were heavily popular for their quality. His employees were happy with the management and my friend had everything working in his way.

But he was neglectful about one thing: filing returns and paying taxes. He never paid much attention to it as he had an accountant to whom he handed over all the responsibilities about these things.

In October 2011, when he was admiring the beauty of the regal mountains of Shimla, he received a message from the bank stating that a check which he had previously issued had bounced. He felt a little confused but didn't pay much heed to it.

Two days later, when he returned home from a lovely vacation, he had a letter waiting for him in his mailbox. It was from the Income Tax Department of India.

The income tax notice stated that he needed to pay Rs 80 lakhs as the tax for the income of his company in the fiscal year 2006-2007 along with other penalties. It came to him as a huge shock as he had not earned the amount of money in that fiscal year on which Rs 80 lakhs can be charged as the tax.

Due to the notice, all his company accounts, as well as his personal accounts, were seized. And it affected his business directly. Sales went down; so did profit. Confused about what to do, he turned to his lawyer for suggestions. The lawyer advised him to bring all the documents on the returns filed for the year 2007-2008 and asked him to file an appeal in the Income Tax Court.

On thorough scrutiny, they found anomalies in the filing of returns. His negligence and the incompetence of his accountant had led him into this mess. After winning the case in the Income Tax Court, he was exempted from the taxes and banks lifted the seizure on his accounts. However, the incident had affected his company's reputation. As a result, he had to work hard to revive his success.

I learned an essential lesson that day when he told me this story. I realized that no matter what you do, you should never be casual about taxes. And this is something that you must remember too: to avoid the circumstances that my friend faced.

What happens when you do not pay your taxes and file your returns properly?

As I said, you must be very careful about paying taxes and filing returns if you are an entrepreneur. Though it may seem unfair to pay a percentage of income to the government at the end of a year, you cannot help it. That is the way of a democracy! We have a government "of the people, by the people, for the people."

As a result, it becomes the moral duty of all citizens to pay their taxes and file the returns properly; so that the government can continue its work. Apart from the moral codes, paying taxes and filing returns properly also presents you with several opportunities.

Suppose you are thinking of expanding your business and you need a loan from the bank to do so. If you have filed your returns and paid your taxes properly, then it will not be a problem for your company to receive the loan amount as your credit score likely will be high. Plus, you may be able to enjoy several benefits that the government offers for small- and medium-sized enterprises apart from tax exemptions. Thus, all it requires is your enthusiasm to file the returns within the specified time.

Now in India, the returns must be filed by July 31 of the said fiscal year. But what happens if you miss the date? Well, you will still have three years of time from the original deadline to file the returns properly. However, if you miss that deadline too then you can get into trouble.

If you are concerned about whether you would be jailed for not filing returns or paying taxes properly, then I must say that it is a far stretch. But you can obviously end up like my friend!

It is not wise to miss the deadlines when it comes to income tax and filing returns. It is always better to be on the good side of the tax department. Plus, it is not so difficult to pay taxes and file returns since everyone has an internet connection these days. So, just take a few minutes of your time to get things done properly as you will be the gainer in the end.

Accounting: Everything you must know:

I have already stated the importance of paying taxes and filing the returns by the due date. I have already made it very clear about what can happen if you do not comply with the regulations of the income tax department.

But where does the accounting fit in all this? Why is it so necessary?

Well, the accounting is necessary for your company as per the rules of your country's income tax department. Proper accounting not only helps to keep your financial records correct, such that you do not face any problem while filing the returns, but it also plays a great role when it comes to auditing and furnishing the report from an accountant on your returns.

So, you need to hire or contact an accountant to do this work for you. But that does not imply that you can be carefree. You must be very careful about the records that you are providing to the accountant, and you must always cooperate with your accountant on every matter to set your financial records right.

For example, in India, per the guidelines of the IT department, you must have your accounts audited by an accountant otherwise you will have to pay 1.5% of your total sales or Rs 1,50,000 as a penalty. Moreover, if your company deals in international transactions or some specific domestic transactions then you will have to furnish a report from a chartered accountant. Failing to do so can cost you Rs 1,00,000 as a penalty.

Now, are you getting the picture of why accounting is important?

However, if your company does not require you to publish a report from an accountant then it is better to take matters into your own hands. Yes, you can do it yourself. So, it will not only save you a lot of money but it will also provide you with an idea of your income as well as expenditures.

Back when I started my company, I had an accountant to do the job for me. However, it created a lot of problems as I needed to provide my accountant with all the documents and records so that she could do her job perfectly. Plus, I had to recheck everything that she did to make sure that no discrepancies existed in the records.

One day while I was talking to my mentor, he said: "Why are you spending so much on an accountant?"

"I think that's more convenient. Having an accountant makes the job easy," I replied.

"I don't think so. You still need to check the records and you are very much involved in it," my mentor said.

"Yes, that's true. So, what do you suggest I do?" I asked.

"Well, do it yourself. It will help you a lot," my mentor replied.

As a result, I took matters completely into my own hands and started doing the accounting myself. It helped me to save a lot of money and it was more convenient because I had all the records in the correct manner while compiling the returns.

So, my suggestion to you is, if you feel comfortable, then do the accounting yourself.

What do you need to do for that?

Firstly, you must keep gathering all the receipts and information that are needed to file the return. During tax filing season, it becomes very complicated for tax accountants to gather all the information as they work on several tax files at one time. This can result in unwanted discrepancies while filing returns, which in turn can lead you to trouble. But if you are doing it yourself then you will not have to be worried about these problems.

The second thing that you must be very careful about as an entrepreneur is to be organized. You need to organize all the information in separate folders so that it does not become a problem to find something while tallying the records. But if you hand over a heap of unorganized information to an accountant, it will not only increase the fees but it can also create problems for you. Hence, it is very important to be organized.

Most business people or entrepreneurs make a mistake which often proves to be costly. They leave it to their accountants to categorize and tally the records. As a result, the accountants charge more and there always exists a probability of making unwanted mistakes. So, it is better to categorize all your checks, receipts, invoices and business expenses and tally it all properly. Double-check the calculations and make sure that no incongruity exists in your records.

Still, if you feel unconfident then you can always have it checked by a tax accountant to make sure that you have not made any mistake.

By following these steps, you will have a clear idea about everything that is going on with your business. You will be totally aware of the profits and expenditures of your company. In other words, you will have total control over everything and you will be able to make sure that your company runs in harmony.

It is not necessary to have a degree or credentials to do the accounting for your company. All it takes is the guts to take the matter into your own hands in order to create the difference.

From my personal experience, I can suggest that it will be much easier for you if you do the accounting yourself as it is always good to be totally involved in your own business.

Paying the taxes: A detailed guide

As I have already told you the importance of accounting, it is now time to address the elephant in the room. Yes, it is now time for me to help you understand the taxes that you need to pay as a company.

In India, for example, the month of July is often regarded as the tax month. Yes, you need to pay your taxes and file the tax returns by July 31 of the assessment year. In the USA, April 15 is famous as income tax deadline day.

Thus, we are presented with the very first question. What is the assessment year, or tax year?

The assessment year is basically the fiscal year for which you need to pay the taxes. Getting a little complicated? Well, let me make it easy for you.

In India, the assessment year is the year for which you file the return for the previous year. What does it mean? Suppose you started your company on January 1, 2018. Thus, the assessment year is 2018-2019 whereas the taxable year or previous year is 2017-2018. In India, the taxable year ends on March 31. Thus, if you have started your company on January 1, 2018, then your tax year will end on March 31, 2018. And you will have to pay and file the income tax returns for the tax year on or by July 31, 2018.

So, when you are calculating the taxes you will have to be very careful about two dates. Firstly, you need to remember that the tax year ends on March 31 whereas the assessment year ends on July 31. So, when you are calculating the tax or filing the returns, then you will have to consider the income from April 1 of the last year till March 31 of the current year.

Truth be told, it is more difficult for entrepreneurs to calculate the taxes that need to be paid than an it is for an average employee. But as I always say, the road of an entrepreneur is not a cakewalk; it is full of challenges.

Unlike their employees, most entrepreneurs do not draw a fixed salary. So your taxes will be calculated on the basis of the profit and gains of your company.

For a company in India, you will have to pay Goods and Services Tax or GST for the products or services that you offer. And that must be in compliance with the income tax returns in order to avoid any problem.

Now, let us calculate the income tax that you need to pay for your company. As per the tax slabs mentioned in the Income Tax Act of 1961, if your company's income varies from 0 to 1 Crore Rupees in a year then you will have to pay 25% of your income as income tax. However, if your income exceeds 1 crore but is lower than 10 crores then 25% of your income along with a 7% surcharge on your income will be levied as the income tax. If your income exceeds 10 Crore then you will have to pay 12% surcharge along with the basic income tax. Lastly, for companies with income exceeding 50 Crores, the income tax rate is 30%. Basically, no matter how much profit you make, you will have to pay income tax on it.

Also, many governments, including India's, keep changing the tax rate for companies every year. So, it is always wise to keep a close eye on these rates.

Here, one thing you must remember! In India, you can claim a return of 10% of the payment that you receive from your clients as TDS. TDS stands for Tax Deducted at the Source. Now, it is easy for the salaried employees to claim TDS as it is generally fixed by the employer. In the case of entrepreneurs, you can claim TDS too on the payments that you receive. The gross income subtracted from 10% of the payments that you have received from your clients is your taxable income.

Plus, there are some other cess and surcharges levied on companies in India. It is best to check the website of the your country's tax department to have a better understanding of such charges. You also need to keep an eye or your local income taxes, if there are any.

Now that I have helped you to understand the basic calculation of the income tax, it is time for me to take you to the next step: how to pay the taxes.

I have already informed you that March 31 marks the end of a tax year in India. So, if you pay the tax before that date then it will be deemed an advance payment of the income tax. You can do this in a quarterly manner. However, if you pay the tax after the date, then it will be deemed as the self-assessment tax and there will be some additional taxes added to the amount.

Hence, it is always better to pay the taxes in advance. It saves you from additional charges and makes it easy to pay the taxes without any hassle.

The advance payment of taxes starts from June 15 on a quarterly basis. So, you will have to pay your advance taxes on June 15, September 15, December 15 and March 15, at amounts specified by the government. Thus, you will have a lot less headache about paying taxes and you will not have to hurry at the end of a financial year.

The best thing to do is to have all the information at your fingertips as I have mentioned before. Plus, you will have to estimate your future income. Just total the amount and then calculate your tax liabilities in a proper way so you will not have to face any hassle.

The great Greek philosopher **Plato** once said: **"When there is an income tax, the just man will pay more and the unjust less on the same amount of income."**

Well, you will not have to pay more or less. Just audit your gross income, profits and expenditures properly to pay the tax that is accurate for you.

Paying taxes properly not only helps you to avoid any problem, it also takes the country ahead. So, you must never back away from making the necessary effort to help your country to develop further.

Filing tax returns: A crucial job:

Now, we are at the most critical stage of the chapter. I will now tell you about filing the tax returns in detail.

Your responsibility does not end at just paying the taxes. You will have to file the tax returns. Contrary to popular myths, filing the returns is as important as paying the taxes.

Whether you have a private limited company or a one-person company, it is necessary to file the returns otherwise you may be penalized.

Before we proceed to the details, let me recap the penalties that you may face in India if you fail to file your returns accurately.

As per the Companies Rules of 2014, the government has mandated the filing of the returns for companies at the end of the assessment year, that is by July 31. You may face a penalty of 50,000 rupees up to Rs 5 lakhs on failing to do so. Furthermore, as the director or owner of your company, you may face an imprisonment of six months along with the penalties if you do not file your returns. So, now do you understand how serious this matter is?

If you fail to file the returns for three years in a row then you can be disqualified by the government from running your company or starting any other company for at least five years.

And other severe legal actions can be taken against you and your company. Hence, it is very important that you file the taxes properly. Whatever country you are located in, you need to be aware of the possible penalties for failing to file.

In the earlier days of my entrepreneurship, I had the pleasure of meeting a director of a private limited company. As I was young and did not have confidence, I naturally asked him to guide me about filing tax returns.

When I broke the topic to him, he was shocked and burst into a laugh.

He told me, **"Do not bother about these things. Just enjoy the perks of being an entrepreneur."**

Well, it was partly good advice as it is so important to enjoy the work you do. However, I did not like his negligence about filing tax returns.

After a few years, I received news from an acquaintance that the respected director was serving a few months in prison for not filing the returns of his company along with paying heavy penalties. Plus, he has been disqualified for eight years by the authorities from serving as a director in any company.

Though the news was not so pleasant given that I knew that person, somewhere deep down I was pleased with myself. Maybe it was for trusting my instincts more than putting my faith in the advice given by someone incompetent.

You can now understand why I have given this topic such importance.

You probably know that you need to fill out an Income Tax Return form or ITR form to file your returns in India. But which ITR form is applicable for your company? This is something that you need to find out first.

Well, if you have a partnership firm then you will have to choose the ITR-4 form for your business. Actually, this form is used by all types of businesses that fall under the list of businesses specified under Section-44AD as well as Section-44AE of the Income Tax Act of 1961.

Furthermore, if your company is a limited liability partnership, a body of individuals or an Association of Persons, then you will have to fill out the ITR-5 form as per the guidelines mentioned in the Income Tax Act of 1961.

Of course, now it is time to have a look at the ITR-6 form. This is the most common form that companies in India use to file their tax returns. So, if your business is not eligible for the above categories then you will have to file your returns with this form. However, if your business falls under the categories mentioned in sections 139(4A) or 139(4B) or 139(4C) or 139(4D) or 139(4E) or 139(4F) of the Income Tax Act of 1961 then you will have to go for ITR-7.

Now, let me tell you about the documents that you will need to file the returns of the company. First of all, you need to have a digital signature. Secondly, you will need your Aadhar number and PAN details of your company. So, it is must that you create a PAN card for your company. Once your company is formed, you will have to apply for a PAN card with form 49AA along with the registration certificate of your company.

Once you have filed your tax returns on the correct form, you will have to take the printout of the ITR-V form or Income Tax Return Verification form from the website of the Income Tax Department and send it after signing to the IT office in order to validate your filed returns.

On an important note, you can also add proof of investment, long-term savings and other proofs to avail tax exemptions.

As the American historian and writer **Albert Bushnell Hart** said: **"Taxation is the price which civilized communities pay for the opportunity of remaining civilized."**

So, it is mine, yours and everybody else's duty to file the taxes properly. It helps the country to grow and develop. Above all, it helps you to run your business successfully without having to face any trouble.

Pay the taxes properly, whatever country you are in, and keep enjoying the perks of being an entrepreneur.

SECRET 9

Be organized, maintain your financial records and file the taxes on or before July 31, or whatever deadline is applicable, to avoid any trouble.

So, what is your strategy to deal with income tax?

10

OUTSOURCING TASKS, MONITORING SOFTWARE AND IP CAMERAS

As the world around us evolves, companies must evolve with it. I have always said that businesses today need to adopt new technologies and processes in order to function properly. You can no longer rely on century-old business techniques and hope to achieve success.

With the development of technology and marketing tools, new types of work have been created which help businesses find a competitive edge. But that does not necessarily mean that you need to hire full-time experts to get these jobs done. You can outsource the work to freelancers or specialized individuals and get the work done in a short amount of time as well as at affordable prices. The practice is called outsourcing and it is one of those techniques that help your company to grow without having to handle less important affairs.

I have also stressed the importance of a proper work culture and discipline in the office. However, the digitalization of the world has created several distractions for workers today.

We often find our employees checking Facebook or watching YouTube while wasting the precious time of the company. This type of reckless behavior can reduce the operational efficiency of your company.

"Why is discipline so important in our lives?"

This is one question that always made me think since I was a child. But I never got a proper answer. However, as I started walking down the path of life and gained experience, I became sure of one thing. I understood that proper discipline and work culture help us to move forward in our lives. Hence, another thing became very clear to me: that I need to live a disciplined life in order to achieve success. Only by becoming disciplined can we be successful.

"To enjoy good health, to bring true happiness to one's family, to bring peace to all, one must first discipline and control one's own mind. If a man can control his mind he can find the way to Enlightenment, and all wisdom and virtue will naturally come to him." This is something **Lord Buddha** preached to his disciples more than 2,500 years ago. And every word of this quote is still relevant to this day.

However, I never realized the value of being disciplined in real life before establishing my own start-up. It had never occurred to me how important this philosophy actually is. But I got a glimpse of hope once I started my own company. It wasn't easy to keep my employees disciplined all the time; especially when we used to fail.

That was when I understood that I need to be nifty! It became fully understandable that I could not persuade my employees to become disciplined by forcing them. I needed to be the person who comes up with nifty tricks and uses surveillance tactics as that was the only way to make my venture successful.

The thing that employees need to understand is that the interest of the company is much more important than individual interests. The company is much bigger than any one person. It is your duty to put this concept into their brains. And every second they waste watching videos or using social media, the company loses an opportunity.

Being an entrepreneur is not about the privileges you enjoy rather it sometimes becomes like managing children. So, you need to be crafty and make use of the resources available to make sure that your employees do not waste precious working hours in doing something non-productive.

Outsourcing tasks: Why do you need to start it now?

In the recent times, the term outsourcing has become very significant. As technology and marketing tools develop today, several new types of work have surfaced.

Most companies today use their website to draw the attention of their customers. And the term SEO (search engine optimization) has thus become very important as it offers you the chance to help your website rank high in the Google search engine results.

However, the success of the SEO of your website depends largely on its content. Content is one of the most important things that make your website engaging to your clients. Thus, your company needs the aid of a professional content writer to produce quality content.

Now, if you hire a full-time content writer then you will have to provide a fixed salary at the end of every pay period even if they do not need to write anything in that time. Plus, you will have no immediate recourse if the quality of the content drops suddenly. As a result, you will become the loser ultimately.

It will not be the case if you outsource your job to freelancers. With the blooming of digital marketing, the number of freelancers in the market today has increased rapidly. Several freelancing platforms have also been created to allow you to connect with freelancers directly.

You can work directly with a freelancer or utilize the platforms available to get your work done. And the best thing about this practice is that you actually reduce the expenditure of your company greatly.

For example, when you are contacting a freelance content writer to work on a project for you, you will only have to pay on the basis of the number of words written. Yes, normally, the payments to a freelance writer are made on a per word basis.

And you do not need to pay an extra penny to anyone. It saves you a lot of trouble. You get your work on a specified deadline without actually having to go through any hassle.

As you know, my company offers website development, hosting and digital marketing services. So, my company really requires content writers and banner designers for several purposes.

During my early years as an entrepreneur, I had permanent content writers as well as designers in my team. However, the experience was not fruitful at all. Firstly, I had to pay a respectable salary to the writers and designers even though the work was scarce.

Plus, I never used to get the work within the specified deadlines. And when I would rush them to deliver the work then I would be provided with something very poor in quality. This continued for a few years until my mentor made me realize that my approach to these things was wrong.

One day, I was sitting in my mentor's office and talking to him about certain matters.

Suddenly, he asked me: **"Abdul, do you still have your permanent writers and designers in your office?"**

"Yes sir, they are still there," I replied.

"And how is that turning out for you?" he asked.

"Well, they are really troublesome to deal with. But I think they will come around," I said being unconfident.

"Why are you fooling yourself, Abdul? You also know that there are some things that never work. How much leniency and patience are you going to show? You are hurting your business by doing this," my mentor said in disgust.

"So, what can I do, sir?" I asked him in search of a definitive solution.

He smiled and said: **"Outsource your work, son! The internet has provided us with the opportunity to outsource work to freelancers and it is really much more cost efficient. Outsource your work and you will never have to deal with these problems again."**

I listened to him!

Since then I have been outsourcing the content and banner design to freelance workers. And the results that I have received are extraordinary. Now, I get my work by the due date and it has actually helped me to adhere to my business goals as well as to prosper.

Running a company does not imply that you will have to have an employee for all the work that your company requires. Smart entrepreneurs always extend the domain of their work with clever outsourcing.

As the American journalist **Larry Elder** once said: **"Outsourcing and globalization of manufacturing allows companies to reduce costs, benefits consumers with lower cost goods and services, causes economic expansion that reduces unemployment, and increases productivity and job creation."**

Well, the quote briefly describes everything that I have said so far. By outsourcing certain jobs, you are providing an opportunity for someone to earn money while you are reducing the expenditure of your own company. It is undoubtedly a clever technique that every entrepreneur must utilize.

So, use the freelancing platforms or contact a freelancer, give them work and pay only for what they are doing. This way, you will be able to save a lot of money and steer your business to the peak of success.

Managing software for staff monitoring: Why do you need it?

In the world today, technology is developing at a rapid rate. Modern technologies have made the world a better place and our lives have become much easier.

Every sector is depending largely on modern technologies to move forward. Then why won't you invest to implement the latest technologies in your business? With the help of technology, you will not only be able to increase operational efficiency but it will also increase the productivity as well as the individual efficiency of your employees.

As early as the 1980s, scholars found that modern technology was helping companies to boost their productivity and helping their employees to work with discipline and achieve success; a new social order was developing with no room for inefficiency. And this observation is becoming more and more apropos with the passage of time.

Yes, we all strive for efficiency. We all want to be highly effective. We want to reach the peak of success for which being efficient is essential. Thus, efficiency is something that we need to achieve these days. Well, it can be easily achieved with the help of modern technology.

The success of an organization depends largely on the efficiency of its employees. If your employees are not productive enough, if they are inefficient, then it is never possible for you to achieve the success that you aim for. Though it is true that you can hire only efficient individuals and train them to increase their efficiency further, it does not always serve your purpose. It does not ensure that your employees will become highly productive.

The only way you have to ensure utmost productivity for your employees is to implement the latest technologies in your business.

And technology also helps you to ensure that your employees are working efficiently.

Though technological developments have made it easier for people to live more comfortably, it has also provided people with more distractions. Most entrepreneurs these days complain about how employees are wasting their precious work hours to play games, watch YouTube videos or check out their Facebook accounts on their office computer. And it is really becoming a problem for employers.

It is destroying the work culture within the company and making the employees less productive as well as inefficient. As a result, it has become very important for business owners to find a cure for this problem.

While many companies take radical steps like blocking websites such as Google, Facebook, Twitter, YouTube and others in their company server in order to prevent employees from accessing the sites, I prefer a much subtle approach.

I prefer to use employee monitoring software to have an eye on the activities of my employees all the time. Employee monitoring software is an expansive technology that helps you to control the activities of your employees during work hours.

The software helps you to track every movement of your employees and see what they are doing. Apart from monitoring, the software also helps you to take appropriate actions against the employees who are too much inclined towards distractions.

The software has several functions. Firstly, it helps you to understand the time efficiency of your staff. The software provides you with a detailed report which shows how much time the employees utilize to finish their work. It also helps you to keep an eye on the employees whose activities seem suspicious.

Furthermore, the employee monitoring software takes periodical screenshots of the screen of your employees. Thus, you will always know what they are doing. From the apps that are being launched to the devices that are being connected to the system, you will be able to keep track of everything with the help of this software. Lastly, the software is highly intelligent as it stops working as soon as your employee stops working.

Everything cannot be achieved by persuading or forcing the staff. You need to be tricky as well as innovative while dealing with your employees. It is the only way to achieve success as an entrepreneur.

I had faced similar problems with my staff. I knew that my employees were wasting time during valuable work hours by surfing the internet or going on social media. However, I had no way of proving this as I could not just blame any employee randomly without solid proof.

As these things continued, the productivity of my company started to decrease and my company was failing to make good profits. I was becoming more and more frustrated with my staff but there was hardly anything I could do to stop these practices in my office.

Luckily, I came across a blog post regarding employee monitoring software one day and it really turned the tables completely. I had the software installed on my company server and it gave me full access to monitoring the activities of employees in detail.

From the emails that they were sending to the applications that were being launched in their computer screen, I would get periodic notifications about the activities of the employees with screenshots. The software also provided me with detailed reports from a specified date range showing the time efficiency of my employees.

So, I started confronting the employees who were extremely less productive and inefficient with a detailed report of their harmful practices. I made them understand everything that they were doing wrong. And if somebody still failed to adhere to the ethics of the company, I fired them to keep my workforce completely efficient.

It really changed the atmosphere in the office. The employees who used to waste their precious time in fulfilling their selfish desires were readily transformed into an efficient workforce. This boosted the productivity of the company greatly and we climbed back to the peak of success again.

Now, my employees know that they are being monitored all the time. Thus, it fuels them with a new zeal to prove themselves in front of me by completing their individual work efficiently.

Though it may sound like I am breaching the privacy of my staff, it is not the case. I am simply doing what needs to be done to keep my employees disciplined. As an entrepreneur, I consider myself as the patriarch of my company and all the members of my staff are like my children. So, it is my duty to show them the right way, to motivate them and to make them disciplined as long as they are within the confines of the office.

Thus, do not force your will on your employees. Use employee monitoring software, monitor every activity of your staff during work hours and make them understand their faults with the detailed report that the software provides. That is the only way you can truly become successful in the world of entrepreneurship.

IP cameras: A simple way to monitor the office and remote locations

"What is new about installing cameras? And why do I need these special cameras?"

This was the first question that I asked my friend when he told me about the IP cameras. Installing cameras within the confines of an office is nothing new. So, I could not understand what the fuss is all about.

I was eager to know and it was quite obvious from the look on my face. My friend could not control himself and he burst out into laughter.

It made me somewhat angry and I said: "Why are you laughing? Now, tell me about the IP cameras."

My friend somehow controlled himself and said: "**Well, the IP camera is a special type of camera that provides you with the opportunity to monitor the activities of your employees in real time. And the best part about these toys is that you will be able to control it from your home without any hassle. It will help your staff too. Install them in all your offices and you will understand how good these cameras are.**"

I was pretty convinced by what my friend said, and the prospects of the camera really intrigued me. Well, the rest is history but I think you get the picture.

So, the story gives you an idea of what the IP camera is and how it helps you. But still, there are several questions in your mind. Well, let me clear up your confusion once and for all.

Honestly, it is fair to say that the IP cameras are the future of the CCTV system. The analog CCTV systems which were used widely before the development of the IP cameras were very problematic. Firstly, the analog CCTV cameras had a bad picture quality and it was very hard to recognize someone using those cameras. Furthermore, they were not wireless and thus companies need to have someone to monitor the entire surveillance process. Plus, the space covered by the analog cameras was too narrow which created several problems.

However, the IP cameras have successfully eradicated all these problems and they have established themselves in the market as a useful tool for entrepreneurs. The best thing about the

IP cameras is that the picture quality that they offer is much better as compared to the old CCTV cameras.

As a matter of fact, the picture resolution of most of the IP cameras starts from 20MP and they generally offer HD quality footage. As a result, you will have a clear view of all the activities that are going on within your office confines. Plus, these advanced cameras cover a large space. So, you will not have to install a camera in every corner of your office.

But the most intriguing thing about the IP cameras is perhaps the fact that they are wireless and you can control them remotely. So, it saves you the trouble of recruiting someone to do the surveillance job for you.

Now, you may ask about the importance of this camera in an office space. Obviously, you can install the employee monitoring software in your system to track every activity of your employees on their computer. Then what is the need for the IP cameras?

Well, the tracking ability of the employee monitoring software is limited to the computers of the employees. But they can also access the internet, social media and other platforms on their personal mobile devices or laptops. And there is no way you will be able to track their activities. Thus, the IP cameras are needed.

Plus, the cameras enhance the security of your office greatly. With these cameras, you will be able to check whether anyone is getting involved in any unacceptable activity. You will always have your eyes on every little detail of your office.

Moreover, the IP cameras not only help the employer, they help the employee too. If an employee has lost a valuable item then they will be able to check the footage from the cameras installed in the office to find it. So, it is fair to say that the IP cameras make your office much more secure.

Above all, these special cameras provide you with the option to continue the surveillance from your home. You do not need to visit your office. You will be able to monitor everything from your smartphone while sitting on your couch.

This is especially helpful for companies with multiple offices in different locations. You will not have to go on a surprise visit to your remote offices to have a good look at the activities of your employees as you will be able to have an eye on them always with the IP cameras.

So, install the IP camera in all your offices and let it become your eyes and ears.

SECRET 10

Outsource certain jobs and reduce your company's expenditure while improving its productivity greatly.
So, what is your strategy to increase the productivity of your company?

11

BUILDING SUCCESSFUL TEAMS AND REDUCING WORKPLACE NEGATIVITY

"Always have a positive attitude towards every-thing. Never let negativity foster. Harbouring resentment and negative attitude will result in your downfall" – I was taught these simple lessons by my father as a child.

Whenever my father passed his wisdom to me, it used to make me happy. Though I did not understand everything that he said, it simply made me happy to hear my father's doting voice. But I did not forget what he said either and his words guided me to the right path later in my life.

Now, I fully understand what my father meant by advising me to never t harbor negativity in my mind. Negative emotions and feelings never do anything good to anyone. Negativity demotivates you from doing any work; it prevents you from achieving success as well as growth and most importantly, negative feelings distance you from the people surrounding you.

"Every day we have plenty of opportunities to get angry, stressed or offended. But what you're doing when you indulge these negative emotions is giving something outside yourself power over your happiness. You can choose to not let little things upset you" – this memorable quote is from the famous American televangelist **Joel Osteen** on one one of his shows. And it actually gives you a clear idea why it is essential to dispose of all the negative emotions.

Negativity doesn't just trouble individuals. Workplace negativity is one of the biggest problems that entrepreneurs face. The rise of negativity among employees jeopardizes the company's business processes and prevents business growth. It is one of the biggest problems in the work environment of today. Lack of proper leadership, employee conflicts, resentment towards the management and several other reasons contribute to the rise of this problem.

The success of any organization depends on the teamwork. Thus, entrepreneurs today are putting their efforts into building teams which can work in perfect harmony and take the company to the peak of success. However, the rise of workplace negativity conflicts with the team building efforts. Yes, workplace negativity poses a great threat to the working of the organizational teams which in turn harms the company.

As I have said in previous chapters, conflicts and negativity result in the failure of a company. Be it ego clashes among the employees, employee nature, resentment towards leadership and management or anything else, conflict and negativity among employees can turn your company into a war zone. Even if the problem arises within a team of employees, it can have a significant effect on the efficiency and productivity of your company.

Entrepreneurship comes with a plethora of challenges, as you know. And reducing workplace negativity and building successful teams are two of the biggest challenges that an entrepreneur can face.

However, they cannot be solved by forcing the employees or taking drastic measures. You need to understand any problem that your employees are facing; you need to understand the problems that are giving rise to negativity. Only by contemplating the problems of your staff will you be able to ensure a positive atmosphere in your workplace.

You must always remember that you are the leader of your company. It is your duty to prevent conflicts, resentments and negativity within your organization. Negativity will only increase if you try to force your staff to produce efficient work without understanding their problems, which can be solved only through proper leadership, communication and motivation.

So, it is your prime duty as an entrepreneur to get to the bottom of the problem, listen to your employees and motivate them to reduce negativity, build successful teams and boost the productivity of your company.

Let me tell you about one of my experiences that helped me understand the concept of building teams and reducing workplace negativity.

In my sophomore year as an entrepreneur, I was trying hard to expand my business and adopt new systems and processes to increase sales and provide quality service as well as support to my clients. So, I came up with the plan of creating a dedicated sales team to supervise the entire process of sales.

I handpicked some of my best employees to form the sales team. They were also responsible for providing the customers with proper sales support apart from supervising the sales processes and creating reports. I was sure that this would boost the sales of my company greatly.

I used to collect reports from the sales team and instruct them on everything they needed to do. Despite all my hopes, the sales of the company started to fall at once. I could not understand the cause of the problem.

I felt hopeless and forced my sales team to work properly. I forced them to communicate with the customers, send them offers and discount plans. But nothing worked properly!

I could understand that something was out of rhythm and the employees were not as sincere to me as they used to be. I was really helpless. No matter what measures I took, nothing worked to change the situation.

Unsure and tired, I turned to my mentor for help. He has always been there for me when I need guidance. So, I was sure that he would be able to show me the correct way.

I told him about everything that had happened. He looked serious and did not say a word.

So, I asked, "What will I do now? How will I get rid of this problem?"

He gazed at my face and said: "This is a problem that you have created. You have failed miserably in building the team and that has given rise to negativity among your staff."

I was surprised!

I asked: **"How is it my fault? What did I do wrong?"**

"Well, have you bothered asking for the consent of the employees before assigning them to the sales team? Furthermore, did you ever care about the fact that your employees might have some suggestions for the plan? All you did was to force them to run your errands and your arrogance led to this situation. Entrepreneurship is not about being the boss. It is about being a leader who can lead his company to the peak of success. And you can only achieve that when you listen to your employees, show compassion, acknowledge their work and take suggestions from them. If you just force your decisions upon them then it creates negativity and this type of situation arises," my mentor said angrily.

I was really ashamed. I understood my fault completely and I vowed to make up for it.

Thus, I called for a meeting with the sales team the next day. I asked whether they were happy to work with the team and asked whether they had any problems. I apologized to them for being hasty and for pressuring them. It eased up the situation greatly.

I even provided them with incentives and asked them for suggestions to get rid of this problem. The atmosphere in the workplace changed completely and everything went back to normal within a few days. Moreover, the sales of my company reached a record high within a few months.

It was at that instant I understood how harmful workplace negativity really is to a company. Since, then I have always tried to listen to my employees, take suggestions from them in every matter and motivate them with incentives, gifts and rewards. And that has helped me to achieve success as an entrepreneur.

The role of an entrepreneur is vast. You actually need to be very cautious to achieve success in this path. So, be very careful while building teams and give it your all to prevent negativity from rising among your employees. It is the only way to prosper for your company.

How to deal with workplace negativity efficiently?

I think you have a clear picture of workplace negativity by now. So, it is time for us to move to the next level. Yes, it is now time for you to understand the techniques of dealing with negativity and maintaining a positive environment in the workplace.

The most important thing that you need to understand is that negativity arises when an employer does not acknowledge the employees and does not give them the freedom to make decisions and work freely. Yes, these are the basic causes of negativity among employees.

There are several other causes, such as not providing the employees with proper remuneration or importance. So, you need to be very careful while dealing with your employees. You must always remember that you need to lead them; there is no need to manage the employees as it often leads to the rise of negativity and resentments.

I often hear people blabbering about why it is not wise to give much freedom to employees. According to them, it will ultimately result in your downfall. But they cannot be more wrong as the reality is different completely.

As I have said before, you need to understand that you are an entrepreneur; you are not the caretaker of a zoo. Similarly, it must also be remembered that the employees are not wild animals; they are human beings too. They also have the brain to make decisions and contribute to the growth of a company.

Thus, there must always be a solid relationship forged from trust between you and your employees. If you ignore that fact and become arrogant then you actually fail. When you ignore the will of your employees then the negativity in your workplace rises.

If you think that being the owner of your company gives you the complete right to make every decision and force the employees to abide by your will, when you do not care about theirs, then you will never be able to achieve the success that you dream of. Though it is true that you are the owner of your company, it does not give you with the right to force your decisions upon the employees and not expect the rise of negativity in the workplace.

Of course, it is true that it is my duty as an entrepreneur to look after the well-being of the company. Similarly, it is my duty to respect the ideas of the employees, give them the freedom to make their own decisions and make them feel crucial to the company. If you succeed in making your employees feel positive and inspired then you will never have to worry about the negativity in your workplace.

I also said at the start of this chapter that leadership is the key to prevent negativity from infecting the work environment in your office. So, you must always remember that as an entrepreneur you need to be the leader of your company. You do not need to become a manager as it always creates a distance between the entrepreneur and the employees.

Who is a leader? This is something that you need to understand first.

A leader is someone who inspires people and makes them follow consciously. Great leaders never turn away from others; they walk ahead of everyone while cherishing the bond that they have with employees. Hence, it is always essential to understand that one does not become a good leader by forcing others, but the person who is loved and acknowledged by others can become a great leader.

And you need to become a leader of such caliber. You need to build a proper relationship with every employee and you need to treat them equally. Tricks like micromanaging will never help you to succeed. By establishing an appropriate relationship and acknowledging your employees, you will be able to establish a proper leadership for your company.

But why am I talking about leadership suddenly? Well, if you become a good leader then you will be able to understand the pulse of your staff completely, which will help you to recognize the problem and act quickly if negativity arises within your work environment.

A few years back, I suddenly noticed a change in the behavior of my employees, and the whole ambiance of my office. It was obvious to me that something was bothering them and that resulted in the sudden change.

Though I noticed the change right away, I did not take any immediate action. I thought that my employees were harboring negative emotions towards the company and I was unsure about the cause. So, I planned to observe the situation for a few days to understand the cause of the problem.

But the situation was worsening with every passing day and there was a lot of tension in the air. Suddenly, I had become a villain in the eyes of my employees. But I did not understand the reason behind the change. I was naturally very tense.

It was hampering the different business processes and profitability margin was falling. One day, I was sitting in my study and thinking about the matter when my wife came in with a cup of hot coffee. She noticed right away that I was tense about something.

"What is the matter? Why are you so glum today?" she asked handing me the cup of coffee.

I was engulfed in my thoughts so much that her voice surprised me. I looked at her but did not say anything.

"Come on, tell me! I can see that something is bothering you just by looking at your face," she said again.

"Well, I do not know why the staff members have been acting all weird lately. They are not interested in doing any work and suddenly I feel like a villain in my own company," I replied in a disappointed tone.

"Oh! It was bound to happen," my wife replied in a careless manner.

I was shocked and asked, "Why? Why do you think so?"

"Have you given them increments this year? All of your competitors have already provided their staff with increments. So, it is natural that they will feel resentful and harbor negative emotions against you," she replied.

This simple conversation opened my eyes immediately and I was able to solve the problem efficiently.

Now, what can you learn from this incident, other than the fact that I have an intelligent wife? Well, there are actually two things that you can learn. Firstly, I was able to notice the negativity in the workplace immediately which helped me to solve the problem before it became serious. Secondly, you can understand that negativity can rise in a work environment when you fail to deliver the things that your employees deserve.

So, always be cautious about the way you treat and deal with your employees as it ultimately matters most when it comes to preventing workplace negativity.

Building an efficient work team within your company:

Since you have already learned how to deal with negativity in the workplace, it is now time to learn the tricks to build a successful team in your company.

Teamwork is very important to the success of the company. When the employees cast aside their individual differences, only can then your company climb up the stairs of success. And you play the most crucial role in this team.

Yes, as the entrepreneur you function as the captain of the team. In a team, everything should be balanced properly and all individuals must play their respective roles perfectly in order to increase productivity and optimize business growth. If there is any discrepancy within the team then it will ultimately prevent your business from performing efficiently.

You must always remember that a work team is not much different from a soccer team. All the members must fulfill their own role with utmost efficiency, only then it is possible for your business to reach its goals.

So, the very first thing that you need to understand while building an efficient team for your company is that you need to inspire your employees to set aside their differences.

You already know from a previous chapter how harmful staff conflict is to your business. You also know that staff conflict prevents your employees from working in harmony with each other which in turn disturbs the teamwork within your organization. So, you must always be very cautious about the clashes and conflicts between your employees while building a team. If there is any problem between two individuals or within a group then you must take the necessary actions to resolve the matter.

One of the most common problems that give rise to conflicts, and the biggest hurdle while building a team, is the ego of the employees. I have said before that ego is the root of all evil. It prevents employees from working with each other efficiently and ultimately creates an imbalance within the team.

Especially, it creates problems among colleagues and destroys the harmonious ambience within the workplace. So, it must be your foremost priority to make sure that there are no ego clashes among the employees. As the leader of the team, you must always be prepared to handle any adverse situation to ensure that the teamwork remains intact.

Secondly, you need to understand the importance of good communication in building a team properly. Communication is undoubtedly one of the most crucial things in any team. If the members of the team do not communicate properly among themselves then it is not possible for the team to provide the best performance.

Let me provide you with an easy example to help you understand the concept clearly. Lionel Messi is respected by soccer fans everyone for his brilliance as a player. However, soccer is a team game and no matter how brilliant players are, they cannot perform well if they are not assisted by teammates. And communication plays a key role in all of this.

Sound communication between Messi and his teammates allows them to play brilliantly on the field. It is the magic of proper communication that allows other players to understand where they need to pass the ball so that Messi can place it inside the goal. If a lack of communication arises within the team then the players will not be able to play efficiently and even the brilliance of Messi will not be able to save his team from losing.

The same can be said about a business team. If your team members do not communicate among themselves then the team will not able to perform in the way they are meant to do, and your business will face losses. Even if you are a good leader, if you fail to establish sound communication within your business team then you will never be able to achieve success.

The next thing that plays an important role in the success of a team is the relationship between you and your employees. If any tension exists between the employer and the employees then a team can never act perfectly. As an entrepreneur, you are the de facto leader of the work team. So, if you do not share a harmonious relationship with your employees then your team building efforts will never actually be fruitful.

To be honest, the relationship that you share with your staff members actually determines how dedicated they are towards the well-being of the company. If your workforce shares a good relationship with you then they will automatically feel engaged with your company and it will enhance their teamwork greatly. However, if a relationship lacks trust, compassion and other such virtues then automatically it becomes weak. Thus, you fail miserably to build the team.

But that situation can easily be averted with proper efforts from your end. If you communicate with your employees, listen to what they want to say and take suggestions from them about different matters then they will automatically start feeling engaged with your company.

However, there is something that must be covered properly before I move forward with the matter.

How important is the relationship between the employer and employees for building an efficient team? This is something that needs to be addressed first before we move on to the next part.

You already know that management authors define employee relations, or the relationship between the employer and employees, as a concept which is used to explain the physical, emotional, practical and contractual relationship between any employer and the employees in an organizational setup.

Thus, it is very important to have a constructive relationship with your employees. And you already know that when the relationship between an entrepreneur and employees is forged from mutual respect, trust, transparency and appreciation, then this is called constructive employee relations.

Obviously, this is something every entrepreneur tries to achieve in order to build a successful team. However, if the relationship between the employer and employees is formed from distrust, fear or disrespect and lack of transparency, then it is called destructive employee relations which must be avoided at any cost within an organizational setup.

"**You can take a team of absolute all-stars in terms of their native abilities, but if they are not working together, they are much less effective than a team where there is less native ability but a higher degree of teamwork and cohesion**" – this is something that the Canadian business tycoon **Stewart Butterfield** said. And I agree with him completely. No matter how excellent your employees are, if there is no sense of teamwork between them then you will never be able to form an efficient team.

Apart from the things that I said above, there are a few other things that you can do in order to build your team efficiently. The main focus of every team is to achieve optimum performance, and there are a few team-building exercises that you can perform to make sure that your team performs at the optimum level.

Once you have resolved the problems among the employees, established proper communication and built a harmonious relationship with your employees, you need to move forward with these simple strategies.

Firstly, you need to set some ground rules for the team. Every team within an organizational setup must abide by a few rules. If a team does not follow any rules then they fail to achieve efficiency and ultimately they fail to realize the business goals. So, you need to identify the requirements of your company and set the rules accordingly such that the team can function properly to achieve those goals.

Plus, you must encourage your employees to brainstorm ideas and suggest new plans for future initiatives of your company. Brainstorming ideas help employees to get more engaged with the company, and it motivates them to work with each other to come up with ideas. Ultimately, it helps in improving the teamwork.

Lastly, you must ensure that the consensus method is used to finalize a plan to avoid any conflict within the team. After setting the objectives and creating the plans, it may take some time for every member of the team to reach consensus.

However, you must allow your employees to reach consensus without forcing your will upon them. By the use of consensus method, you will be able to make sure that the relationship between you and your employees remains on good terms.

It is not easy to prevent workplace negativity and to build an efficient team, but if you take your steps cautiously and patiently then the process becomes much easier.

SECRET 11

*Help your employees to open up about
their feelings by being transparent to them.
It will help you to build a successful team
while eliminating workplace negativity completely.*
So, what is your master plan?

RECAP

I thought of writing this book to help the beginner entrepreneurs to overcome the hurdles and run their business successfully. It comes with ideas, problems and solutions that enable you to face any situation with absolute ease.

So, what do you expect to find in this book? Here, check out;

1. **Inspire them by being you:**
   - Having a sound communication is the best way to motivate the workforce.
   - Listen to your employees and make them feel connected to help them understand their importance in the organization.
   - Be a leader and learn to lead from the front.

2. **Strengthen your workforce with good pay:**
   - Establish a proper wage scale and make every position valuable.
   - Give your employees bonuses and incentives for hard and efficient work.
   - Increase the salary or make them your shareholders, take every step necessary to retain your top employees.

3. **Employees Are the Key:**
   - Give utmost importance to the ideas that your employees provide you with.

- Understand what your employees need, smart employees or hardworking employees.
- Take the necessary steps to help your employees evolve into extraordinary employees.

4. **Hire slow and Fire Fast:**
- Explain the job properly and only choose the best employees.
- Train your employees well and help them achieve the highest performance.
- Fire the employees that cause troubles and are not team players immediately to retain the operational efficiency of your company.

5. **Staff Conflicts: A great enemy of your company's work culture:**
- Determine the cause of the conflict between employees immediately.
- Talk with your employees, make them understand and take any way necessary to resolve the conflict.

6. **Worry in Business and how to handle it:**
- Understand that worrying does not help to solve any problem, it only makes your mind fatigued.
- Avoid anything that makes you feel tired and worried.
- Wake up early and try brainstorming ideas to increase your productivity. And be sure about everything to get rid of any worry.

7. **Structure your business to run itself:**
- Always prepare for the worst and make the amends necessary to help your business run on its own.
- Make your business processes simple to automate the processes.

- Reward your competent employees with attractive positions to provide your company with a way to run without you.

8. **Maintain records, invest in technology and implement work culture:**

- Always maintain a detailed record of your employees. Record the details of the number of leaves your employees have take and everything else to ensure proper working of your organization.
- Implement advanced technologies like CRM software to make sure that your employee operates the machine efficiently and provide customers with desired services.
- Work hard, motivate your employees and be an example to establish a proper work culture in your organization.

9. **Watch the Numbers and Pay Your Taxes:**

- Paying taxes and filing the tax returns within the specified date help you to continue your business successfully without being placed under the scrutiny of Income Tax Department.
- Take the job of accounting seriously while tallying your income and expenditures. Do it yourself and get the results checked by a professional accountant to avoid any mistake.
- Remember to pay advanced taxes as per government protocol. File the tax returns before the specified date and enjoy great returns on the taxes paid.

10. **Outsourcing Tasks, Monitoring software and IP cameras:**

- Keep your workforce focused on the important tasks. Outsource the auxiliary works and responsibilities to reduce the workload on your employees.
- Make use of monitoring software to prevent your employees from spending precious work hours on social media and internet.

- Install IP cameras in your office and manage it from your phone from remote places to have an eye on your employee's activities.

11. Building Successful Teams and Reducing Workplace Negativity:

- Understand how dire the consequences of workplace negativity are. Workplace negativity destroys your work culture, teamwork and ruins your operational efficiency.
- Take every step necessary to reduce negativity and take necessary team building efforts to create successful work teams.

So, without any further ado, take the necessary steps to make for ensuring a success in your business.

www.ingramcontent.com/pod-product-compliance
Lightning Source LLC
Chambersburg PA
CBHW030626220526
45463CB00004B/1427